Also by Melissa Yuan-Innes

The Most Unfeeling Doctor in the World
and Other True Tales From the Emergency Room

The Unfeeling Doctor, Unplugged

The Unfeeling Wannabe Surgeon

The Unfeeling Doctor Betwixt Birthing Babies

The Knowledgeable Lion

Fifty Shades of Grey's Anatomy

Broken Bones

Your Baby Is Safe *(with illustrations by D. Antonia Truesdale)*

BUDDHISH

Exploring Buddhism in a Time of Grief
One Doctor's Story

Melissa Yuan-Innes, M.D.

Buddhish © 2017 Melissa Yuan-Innes
Second Edition

Cover © 2017 by Design for Writers

All rights reserved.

**Join Melissa's mailing list at
http://www.melissayuaninnes.com/**

Yuan-Innes, Melissa, author
Buddhish / Melissa Yuan-Innes.
(Exploring Buddhism in a Time of Grief
One Doctor's Story)
Issued in print and electronic formats.
ISBN 978-1-927341-73-5 (softcover).
--ISBN 978-1-927341-08-7 (PDF)

To advise of typographical errors,
please contact olobooks@gmail.com.

Published by Olo Books
http://olobooks.com/

In association with Windtree Press
http://windtreepress.com/

For Isadora

and

for those who have loved and lost

Contents

Part I   12

The First Noble Truth	13
The Second Noble Truth	14
The Third Noble Truth	15
The Eightfold Path	16
Right Understanding	17
Right Aspiration	19
Right Concentration	22
Right Action	24
Right Speech	25
Right Livelihood	27
Right Effort	29
Right Mindfulness	31
What Is Buddhism, Anyway?	33
Meditation 1.0	35
The Five Hindrances	36
Aversion	38
Lust	41
Restlessness	42
Doubt	43
Sloth and Torpor	45
Custom Pop Quiz	48
Stress Test	49
Three Poisons	52
Blame (The BMW Story)	55
Forbidden Happiness	57
Yoga	60
Meditation 2.0	62
Dedication	64
Labels	65

Part II: Loving-Kindness and Community   66

Mustard Seeds	67
Openness *(Bodhichitta)*	*70*
Got Nectar?	74
All Mustard Seeds Are One	76
Master Reverend Olo	80
Loving-kindness (Metta)	83
Mindfulness, Part II	85
But I Keep Having These Thoughts ...	88
Mustard Seeds at Work	92
What Is the Sound of One Hand Clapping?	96
Other Pregnant ... Men?	100
Isabel	103
The $86,400 Question	106
Equanimity, Part II	109
May You Be Happy	111
But What About Isadora?	113
Music	115
Permission to Mourn Melissa-style	117
Koan: Loving and Losing	120
Show Me the Pain	122
More Wisdom From Isabel	125

Part III: Creating a New Story   127

Haiku as Mindfulness	128
Is This the Truth?	130
Gentleness	133
Karma & Reincarnation	138
Attachment	143
Enlightenment	145
Accepting What Is	147
Oriental Medicine	149
Creativity	151

Logic vs. Metaphors	154
The Baby Who Saved His Mother's Life	157
Wrestling With the Angel	161
Samsara. Nirvana.	162
Rainbows and Marshmallows	165
Buddhist or Just Buddhish?	168
Cinderella	171
Little Miracles	173
Heal Thyself	180
Epilogue (Meditation 3.0)	183

Appendix: Buddhist Books I Love — 186

Meditation Apps	189
Non-Buddhist But Still-Useful Resources:	190

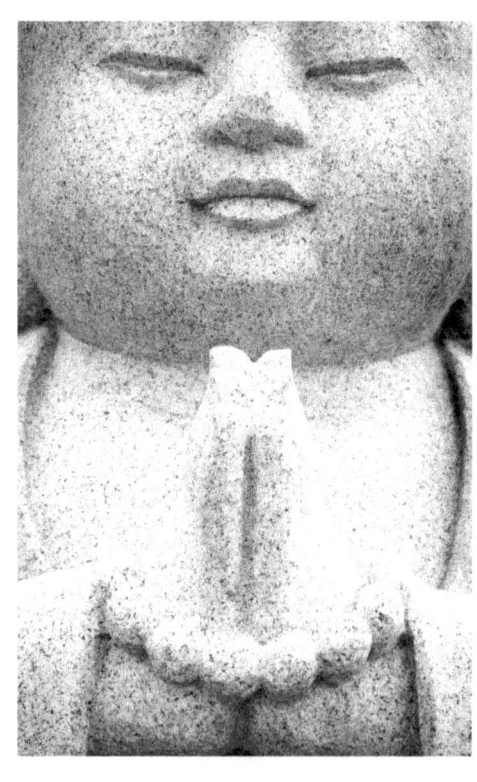

Introduction

I like Buddhism, but I can't say I'm a world-class Buddhist.

"I'm Buddhist-ish," I told my husband, Matt. I imitated my half-Jewish friend who said he was "Jew. Ish," with a little hand waggle on the "ish," meaning so-so.

Matt laughed. *"Buddhish."*

Right. Buddhish.

If Buddhism were a spectrum, like the spectrum of visible light, with Buddhist monks and nuns meditating at the violet wavelength, I'm on the opposite end, tiptoeing around in the orange light.

However, even a few tablespoons of Buddhism helped save my sanity, and I believe it can help anyone become more grounded and open-hearted, especially after tragedy butchers your life.

This is the story of how I plunged into the valley of darkness, and Buddhism was one of my crutches on the way out.

Which is strange, because I was never terribly interested in religion.

My parents were both raised by super-Christians, so they raised us as nothing in particular. "If you want religion, do it yourself," was their M.O. When I was in grade three, I tagged along to my friends' church. I got to be the old lady in the Christmas play (yeehaw), and sang in the choir, but Sunday school was pretty boring. I dropped out.

One of my grade seven vocabulary words was "agnostic," which suited me perfectly. I didn't know if God existed and didn't think you could prove it either way. "Fence-sitter," said one of my friends, and I agreed.

Until my life shattered as an adult.

I had finally started practicing medicine as a full-fledged emergency doctor. I was 12 weeks pregnant, and I couldn't feel the baby moving. This was before bedside ultrasounds were commonplace in the ER, especially in the underfunded Quebec medical system. So naturally, I ordered blood tests on myself and whipped out the fetal Doppler on my own stomach. I couldn't hear any fetal heartbeat, and my B-HCG test seemed low normal.

I freaked. I was sure I'd had a missed miscarriage, which meant that the fetus had died without any outward signs like bleeding. My hospital's radiology department squeezed me in for a proper ultrasound the next day. Before the ultrasound tech could say a word, the baby wiggled its arms and legs at me.

I burst into tears. The tech chided me because she couldn't get proper images with me weeping, but I loved this baby already, and now I could finally relax.

Then at 20 weeks, I delivered a stillborn baby girl.

We named her Isadora Jane. We buried her ashes. And I tried not to lose my mind.

Since Quebec is Canada's most socialist province, its physicians' association offers eight to twelve weeks of maternity leave to all mothers of stillborn children, defined as 20 weeks to term. I could have refused it and gone back to work, but I knew I needed some semblance of sanity first. I could not look after anyone else when I barely understood how or why I should still be alive.

Winston Churchill said, "If you are going through hell, keep going."

I was in hell. I kept going. But I needed guidance.

I felt like a mother, but not a mother. I was a doctor, but not a doctor who was practicing. I was agnostic, so I couldn't even pretend my baby was in heaven.

I was just messed up.

I went to see the local priest. This is not as weird as it sounds for an agnostic. We'd moved to the country outside of Montreal, and there was a church at the end of our road. Father Dan was cool. He jogged around our neighborhood, often accompanied by a local dog, and a few weeks before, he'd knocked on our door to say hi.

He listened to my story and said, "You need to forgive yourself, and I can't help you with that." He paused and added, "I knew a man who accidentally ran over his three-year-old daughter. He had to forgive himself. But he was the one who had to do it."

This helped enormously. Now I had a goal: forgiveness. But how should I achieve it? It wasn't like getting an A on a test, which was much easier for me.

I rummaged through the grief and self-help shelves at the Cornwall library and unearthed Sylvia Boorstein's *It's Easier Than You Think*. She wrote about a 40-year-old woman dying of cancer who said, "I'm a better and wiser person because of this cancer. But I'd rather not have cancer."

Bingo. I loved the honesty of it. Yes, Isadora's death could make me a better person. But I'd rather have my baby.

I picked up the book and stumbled into Buddhism.

Part I

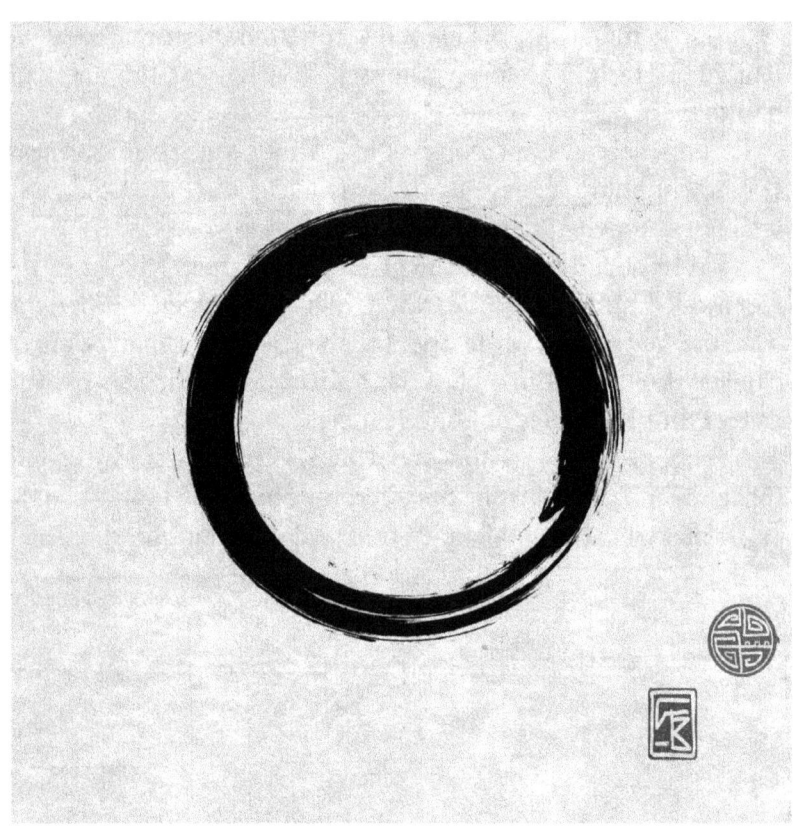

The First Noble Truth:

Life contains suffering.

Perfect. No sugar-coating. You're alive? Not everything will turn out the way you want.

>Isadora died.
>I was suffering.
>I turned the page.

The Second Noble Truth:

Craving causes suffering.

I understood the concept.
  I craved my child.
  I longed for her. I clung to her. I wept for her.
  And yep, I was still suffering.
  I turned the page.

The Third Noble Truth:

Stop craving and you can stop suffering.

I knew that if I could let Isadora go and forgive myself, I wouldn't suffer as much.

But how could I do that? How could I say, "Hey, no problem, my daughter's dead"?

I turned the page.

The Eightfold Path

Also known as the Fourth Noble Truth

Eight things you should try to do simultaneously. No pressure.

> Right Understanding
> Right Aspiration
> Right Concentration
> Right Action
> Right Speech
> Right Livelihood
> Right Effort
> Right Mindfulness

I tried to wrap my head around the eightfold path by translating these puppies into my own idiosyncratic, "Buddhism for doughheads" version that follows. Mostly, it was easier if I didn't think about Isadora, but about the rest of my life.

Right Understanding

Everything changes. Good and bad. That's what you're supposed to understand.

Or as the great TV show *Six Feet Under* put it, "Everything. Everyone. Everywhere. Ends."

That made sense.

My family moved to Frankfurt, Germany, for two years. When I returned to my former school for grade eight, the boys called me "bag lady" and threw spitballs at me, while the girls gossiped and drew cartoons about me.

The most vicious attacker, "Zelda," had been one of my best friends before I moved.

I bided my time for the one remaining year until high school, when I would move on to a more evolved pool of humanity. The end was in sight. Ironically, at our year-end grade eight graduation, Zelda started crying. Her father was being transferred to London, England, so it was her turn to be the new girl in Europe.

Much later, as in a few years ago, she tried to friend me on Facebook. Eventually, I did friend her back, but by then, her invitation had expired.

Everything changes.

Once upon a time, a great king asked for a ring that would make him happy when he was sad and sad when he was happy. The sages made him a ring that said, "This too shall pass."

This too shall pass.

Well, my daughter already passed, to use one of the euphemisms for dying that I'd never particularly liked.

I knew that one day, my heart would no longer be smashed, but I was scared about that, too.

More than anything else, I worried about Isadora. Where was she, now that she was gone? Was she in another realm? Was she just ... dust to dust? Was she here, now, crying, "Mommy, don't let me go"?

Right Aspiration

Life is transience. Got it. My daughter had already transitioned.

Question: What were you supposed to do about that?
Answer: Aspire to be okay with transience.

Sylvia Boorstein said that since the world was always changing, you should try to be like a surfer riding the waves.

Things might be awful or awesome, but you ride it out either way.

Huh. I always wanted to control the waves, or at least control my reaction to them. I would train extra hard! I would study the weather forecast! I would rent the best surfboard!

In real life, I've surfed a few times in Hawaii, but I'm a weak swimmer. In Waikiki once, just after a storm, the waves were powerful, which meant they were easy to "catch" and push you along, but you had to be able to swim out to them, against the tide. Repeatedly.

After our first ride, while I battled my way back to the rest of the group, whom I could hardly see without my glasses, our instructor shook his head and told my husband, "I think your wife has had it."

The Australian guy in our group navigated expertly to my side. "Are you okay?"

"Yup," I gasped, and paddled after him.

I was exhausted. Still, I knew where I wanted to go and what I wanted to do. I'm not strong, but I'm fairly flexible and have good balance from yoga training. Plus I'm super stubborn.

I rode the waves several more times.

So I knew how to surf a little in real life. How should I surf my grief?

Sylvia Boorstein told two helpful stories about Right Aspiration. The first was about a grandmother who stayed angry at her daughter right up until the day she died. She no longer remembered why she was so furious, "but I remember that I am angry."

I've lived that movie. When I was 17, my grandmother looked at me and said, "You look so much like your mother. Just looking at you, I am angry."

This didn't bother me, since any simpleton could tell she and my mother were always sparring. My grandmother and I had never been close. But it meant that I had been marinated in anger from an early age.

Sylvia's second story about Right Aspiration started when she was planting onions with a friend. They anticipated a bumper crop. The friend suggested they give them to the food bank. Sylvia thought, *No, I'll buy you a truckload of onions for the food bank, but these are* my *onions.* Then she took a deep breath and said, "Good idea."

They hadn't harvested a single onion yet, but Sylvia already wanted to hold on to every single one of them. This story made me smile because it was exactly like me and my family. My family loves stuff. Stuff on sale, stuff that's "cute," stuff that's handmade, stuff that's spewed out by a factory overseas. Anything and everything.

Anger. Grudge-holding. Hoarding.

If these were Olympic events, my family could sweep the gold in all three categories.

We didn't surf past them. We clung to them, and we gloried in it.

Gandhi said, famously, "You must be the change you want to see in the world."

So what did I aspire to?
I wanted to honour Isadora.
I wanted her to be safe. I couldn't convince myself she was in heaven, but I wanted her to be safe.
I wanted to forgive myself.
"For what?" my husband, Matt, asked.
"I am the mother. I am the doctor. I should have protected her," I said.
He didn't understand, but I did.

Right Concentration

Captain Cheri Maples, a police officer who has studied Buddhism with the renowned spiritual leader Thich Nhat Hanh, said that her first Zen activity was baseball because it absorbed her concentration (http://bit.ly/zenball).

What does that have to do with religion or philosophy? Not much, on the surface. But I think concentration means you stick with something instead of running from thing to thing.

I had a friend who was always on his way to this fantastic party or texting that amazing friend. Even when he was in front of you, you got the feeling that he wasn't there.

I told him once, "Why are you calling me if you have so much other stuff to do? Just don't call."

He was taken aback, but I wasn't angry, simply matter-of-fact. "I don't care if you call me for one minute. But when you do, I want you to talk to me for that minute."

Of course, I said that before I was lodged in the black hole of grief. Right now, I wanted anyone and everyone to call. But in general, I could see how concentration helped.

The most beautiful description of concentration I ever heard was by the French philosopher, Simone Weil: "Absolutely unmixed attention is prayer."

As Stephen Mitchell, a translator, explained on the public radio show, *On Being*, "In that sense, prayer has nothing spiritual or religious about it. A mathematician working at a problem, or a little kid trying to pick out scales on the piano is a person at prayer ... whether it's inside a church or inside a toy box, [the attention itself is] the quality that is the sacred one" (http://bit.ly/attentionpray).

I could concentrate. Once I sat in my dorm room and said, "I'm not leaving here until I've mastered this section of organic chemistry." I studied for over eight hours in a row, armed with only a glass of water, until the sunlight faded. When I emerged, my apartment mate, Leah, gave me a strange look and told me, "I didn't even know if you were in there or not."

Now, though, I multi-task all the time. It's an occupational hazard. But it's not until I pause in the emergency room for a second that I think, *Oops. What happened to the 'rule out gallstones' woman? Did she get her ultrasound yet?* Sure, the nurse will advocate for the patient (thank heavens), but if I could pay attention to one thing at a time, yet maintain an overall meta-awareness of the emergency room, I would feel less scattered.

I did not want to concentrate on my grief, but I knew that I had to, or it would bite me in the ass.

Right Action

Sylvia wrote, "Act carefully. Everything matters."

When I saw a female patient with abdominal pain, I often did a pelvic exam and took swabs for chlamydia and gonorrhea.

A lot of emergency doctors did not. They would say, *Oh, well, the pain is epigastric* (around the stomach), even when the patient was pointing directly at her vagina. They would order a urine dip, blood tests, and an ultrasound and send the patient away.

I didn't get paid extra to get the patient in a gown, wait for our one gyne room, coach her in the stirrups, grab the Muco gel, and try not to hurt her with the speculum because she was already in pain.

It would be easier and faster to skip the pelvic exam and pretend sexually transmitted infections didn't exist, or to treat on spec (give antibiotics) without the exam. But if I could prevent one case of chronic pain or infertility, I was doing it.

I'm not saying I was a hero, but this was right to me.

The problem right now was, though, I didn't have any clear action to take and nothing felt "right."

What should I do?

What could I do?

Probably nothing.

That felt the worst of all.

Right Speech

I'm pretty good at biting my tongue.

Of course I'm not wise all the time, but for example, I try to avoid bad-mouthing other doctors. Everyone's always trash-talking other physicians in the ER, whether it's this specialist who didn't answer a page or that colleague who screwed the pooch on a diagnosis.

If a patient tells me about a bad experience with a doctor, I listen a little before I tell them, "I can't comment on another doctor's care." I have to say, though, two separate people told me that the same physician fell asleep while taking a patient history. I can't think of how you could give good medical care while asleep.

Even so, in Buddhism, you should wait for someone to ask three times before you give advice, to make sure they're really ready for the answer.

In the emergency room, you have about three seconds to give advice.

Hmm.

Also, in my personal life, I have a tendency to bite my tongue, brood, try to talk to the person in a calm way while s/he continues to wrong me, bite my tongue, try to talk again while still calm, and then just go postal on them.

I have lost a lot of friends this way.

Hmmm.

Two days after I delivered Isadora, I thought I would be okay. I started writing again. I didn't go to sleep clutching the blanket my father had embroidered with her name. I left my handkerchief by the computer. I was going to be all right.

I woke up sobbing.

I tried not to disturb Matt. I'd been waking Matt up every night.

In fact, I'd made up a new rule: only wake him up if you really start bawling.

I began bawling.

He slept on.

I snuggled closer to him.

He woke up and held me.

I described the nightmare I'd had. He hugged me. He consoled me. Then he started to fall asleep while I was still talking.

I had a lot of speech. It might not be the right speech, though.

Right Livelihood

This means, "First, do no harm," i.e., choose a job that does not harm.

That's the first part of the Hippocratic oath. You would think medicine would be a slam dunk in this respect. We Help People. And yet ...

My community hospital is in debt. Beds are closed, or perpetually filled by people waiting for nursing home beds. That means people are stuck in the emergency room, waiting for a bed upstairs. Which means we have no space to see or treat the new people coming hourly (minute-ly?) to the ER. Which means we see people in chairs and/or in the hallway. Which means we're perpetually running. If you work in the system, you know the drill.

As a female doctor, patients would often ask me for a blanket or help to the bathroom. It wasn't what I was paid for. I had a stack of new patients to see and old patients to review. And I kind of didn't know where anything was. (This is usually a guy's tactic. Be ignorant and someone else will take over.)

"It's easier for me to just get the blanket," said my now-doctor friend, Leah. But she did palliative care. She took the time with a few patients instead of managing the masses.

"Help. I need help here. Help. I need to get to the toilet. Help," a patient called, loud and clear.

I tensed. I was writing my orders at the nursing station before I started on the next.

The one nurse covering all of the ambulatory patients was also trying to do a blood requisition.

"Help. I—oh. It's too late."

"Oh, well," said the nurse.

I kept on working too.

Later, I felt terrible.

Right now, I had no livelihood.

I was afraid.

The Quebec medical association was supposed to pay me maternity leave, since Isadora had been over 20 weeks old, but any Quebec administration is capricious in the extreme.

I was worried about the money, but I was more worried that if they turned me down, it meant I wasn't a real mother.

People had also encouraged me to apply for a disability payment, since I carried disability insurance. So now I was one of "those people," asking a doctor to sign a disability form for me.

One of my doctor friends was in mourning and went right back to the emergency room. Later, he confessed, "There were times when people were talking to me, and I had no idea what they were saying. There were times that the nurse took me by the arm and said, 'Dr. Bellomo. This is a prescription. Sign here.'"

I could have gone back to work, but I knew I might very well kill someone. I stayed off.

One week, after walking our dog, I opened the mailbox and found a letter granting me maternity leave, $730 a week for eight weeks.

I burst into tears. Nearly six thousand dollars. Because Isadora was dead.

Right Effort

I was jealous of every pregnant woman I saw. They were living, breathing embodiments of what I wanted and what I couldn't have. I tried to explain it to a friend like, "It's like you're starving and everywhere you turn, you see a sign for a buffet, but you can't go in."

Eight weeks after Isadora's death, I returned to work. Naturally, I tended to pregnant women, listened to their babies' heartbeats, and watched them snap at their other children. "Don't *touch* that, Dakota. I said, *don't touch it!*"

When I told other grieving women online, they were like, "It's normal. Me too. Don't worry about it."

But I did worry about it. I didn't like the anger and the jealousy corroding my veins. Telling myself I was normal didn't help. Telling myself to think kindly thought towards them didn't help.

Matt said, "It's not a zero-sum game. Their pregnancy has nothing to do with your pregnancy."

Didn't help.

I knew I was doing one thing right. If I smiled and pretended nothing was wrong, that I looooved working with pregnant women, that I should switch to obstetrics because I adored it so, I would end up very, very angry.

I did my job and left the exam room as soon as possible. But I couldn't detach from other women's pregnancies.

Fortunately, Buddhism didn't judge me.

Right effort means moving toward wholesomeness. You know what it's like to be kind, generous, and thoughtful. Aim for that. And if you fail, that's okay. No judgment, no cat-o'-nine-tails. Just keep moving in the right direction overall.

It's kind of like a transition toward a healthy diet. You know you should eat more spinach and butternut squash. When you do, you feel good about it. But if you end up eating deep-fried butter one day, well, all right. Aim for better next time.

I remembered a famous Indigenous story where a grandfather said, "I have two wolves battling inside me. One wolf is full of anger, fear, and greed. The other is full love, joy, and kindness. The same wolves fight inside your heart, too."

The grandson said, "But Grandfather, which one will win?"

The grandfather smiled. "The one you feed."

I should add that Buddhism is not into labels. Instead of the "good" wolf or the "bad" wolf, we're all wolves, trying to do our best. But I knew what kind of wolf I wanted to be: the wolf that didn't feel threatened by another wolf's pregnancy.

Right Mindfulness

Years before, at a novel workshop, the writer Dean Wesley Smith castigated all of us for not including concrete sensory details and description of what things looked, smelled, sounded, tasted, or felt like. It made me realize that I'd concentrated on plot and character, but left out this sensory description because I lived in my head all the time.

Instead of right mindfulness, I was into braininess. Medicine is all about memorizing and applying facts and, once you start moving up in the ranks, your ability to perform procedures and make decisions. But no one cares if you notice how a rose smells.

So that weekend, I made a conscious decision to start paying attention to my surroundings.

I re-examined my writing. I'd always included smells. For whatever reason, smells do register on my radar, good and bad. But the other senses, mmph.

My cousin gave me a meditation book that suggested I pay attention to taking a piece of clothing out of my closet, feeling the fabric against my skin and hearing the hangers ring together.

How many times in my life had I yanked on a blouse and run out the door, barely noticing if I had my collar the right way out? (Hint: once one of my classmates straightened the collar of my white coat and said, "You're never too busy to fix your collar.")

In *The Miracle of Mindfulness*, Thich Nhat Hanh said if you paid this kind of intense attention to your own life, it made you wake up and focus, much as if you were driving a car or walking on stilts. Every moment counted.

I realized that after Isadora died, it would have been easier for me to turn to sugar, alcohol, or workaholism than to pay attention to, say, the fact that my milk had come in and I had no baby to feed.

But I was slowly starting to see the judgement and condemnation in my own thoughts. Yes, my baby was dead. Yes, my milk had come in. But Buddhism told me, *Just stay with the fact that your milk is here. That's what's happening right now.*

What Is Buddhism, Anyway?

I don't try to categorize everything, but I found Buddhism extra-hard to classify. I'd always heard it was a religion. "It's not a religion," said one book. "It's a philosophy." "No, it's a science!" exclaimed another.

The Dalai Lama said his religion was kindness. I didn't get that, either. Aren't you a Buddhist, dude (if you can call His Holiness a dude)? Why don't you just say that?

After more reading, I decided that it's not a religion like the other major players because it avoids the whole "my way or the highway to Hell" thing that so turns me off every other form of religion.

In fact, Buddha actively encouraged people to test his theories out for themselves. "As the wise test gold by burning, cutting, and rubbing it, so are you to accept my words after examining them and not merely out of regard for me."

He also explained it like this: "No blind faith is necessary to understand these four Noble Truths."

He didn't say, "Drink my Kool Aid, suckas." He said the equivalent of *Try it out for yourselves and make up your own minds.*

I liked that. I could see how that was a more scientific approach, especially after I read *The Joy of Living: Unlocking the Secret and Science of Happiness,* by Rinpoche Yongey Mingyur.

Also, since proselytizing gives me the heebie-jeebies (I don't even like preaching about smoking cessation or promoting my writing, although I do both), I was pleased that the Buddha said,

"Do not trouble yourself as to whether all or some have realized it [the Truth] or not."

Awesome. I could hardly manage to keep my own head screwed on, let alone try and sway others into the fold. Buddha himself gave me the green light to just concentrate on myself. In fact, that seemed to be the first step.

Buddha didn't ask you to believe in one god or a certain pantheon of gods. In fact, Buddhism didn't seem to believe in God at all. In *Things Fall Apart*, Pema Chödrön called it nontheism. She basically compared theism (believing in a god) to trusting in a cosmic babysitter who's always going to hold your hand, whereas in Buddhism, you figure WYSIWYG (what you see is what you get), so you might as well make peace with death and taxes, 'cause they ain't going anywhere.

Like everything else, Buddhism seemed very mellow on the whole theism thing. You could believe in a god and be a good Buddhist, too. In fact, the Dalai Lama encouraged Westerners to maintain their own religious traditions instead of converting to Buddhism. "All major religions carry the same messages. Messages of love, compassion, forgiveness, tolerance, contentment and self-discipline. I have Muslim friends, Christian friends. All have these same values."

I liked the inherent acceptance, that you could be Buddhist and anything else. It was so common to be Jewish and Buddhist that they had their own nicknames (Ju-Bus or Bu-Jus). It was like having dual citizenship. So I could certainly be Buddhist (Buddhish) and agnostic. Ag-Bu?

Buddha.net summed up "the Buddhist path" as follows:

1. To lead an ethical life
2. To think and act mindfully
3. To develop wisdom

This made perfect sense to me.

Meditation 1.0

However, this also brought me to one thing Buddhism was famous for.

The M word.

Meditation.

Could I really sit down and do nothing?

Could I make myself sit down in a comfortable chair for fifteen minutes?

Okay, ten?

Five?

One?

I wasn't a big meditator. I kind of skipped those parts of the books, just like I clicked past the breathing bits on my livestreaming yoga videos.

I kept reading.

The Five Hindrances

Fortunately, I didn't have to meditate in order to recognize the five hindrances, or mental states that led you away from enlightenment. Sylvia Boorstein called them "difficult mind states."

Pop Quiz Time

Choose your answer and find your favourite hindrance! It's like a *Cosmo* quiz, only it's all spiritual, yo.

Let's say you're a nurse who's been up all night, tending to the sick and saving lives. When you go to the parking lot for a well-deserved rest because you've got another night shift in 12 hours, someone has stolen your truck. You

a) swear profusely, call the police, swear some more, and then start yelling at the security guards;

b) pop over to the car dealership to check out all the new trucks you'll buy with the insurance money (sleep, schmeep);

c) run back into the emergency room, tell everyone there's a thief, and get people all fired up. They work in an emergency room, so everyone's pretty fiery anyway;

d) wonder why the thief picked your truck. Did you park too far away from the streetlights? Did you buy a model that was easy to break into? You should've bought a better alarm system, for sure;

e) go to sleep as soon as you've filed the police report. It's all too friggin' much.

Your Score	
a) Aversion	page 38
b) Lust	41
c) Restlessness	42
d) Doubt	43
e) Sloth and Torpor	45

Aversion

Also Known As Anger or Ill Will

There was once an emergency doctor who liked to yell a lot.

Dr. Loud was short, skinny, and always shouting. If I answered a question wrong, she wouldn't just say so, she would bellow, "BULL*#^@."

So then I'd try again.

"BULL&$#%."

I'd try not to get rattled, take a deep breath, and try a third time.

"BULL!&$#$."

Once a patient threatened a nurse. Dr. Loud got in on the action and swung some punches herself. She sustained two broken ribs, but I imagine she earned some respect too.

When I was in first-year residency (translation: still pretty green), Dr. Loud had a pregnant patient with a vaginal bleed. Dr. Loud paged the OB on call several times, but he was doing a C-section, so she turned on me. "Your job is to go up to OB and stand by the obstetrician. Do not leave his side until he comes down here."

I found the OB writing his operative note. When I explained what service I was on, he frowned at me. "I'll be there as soon as I can. Can she not handle it for a few more minutes?" I wasn't sure what to reply.

The following year, when I was doing ICU call, Dr. Loud started paging me repeatedly. "I can't get a hold of the cardiologist. Look at this electrocardiogram."

I looked. I saw diffuse ST elevation, somewhat like pericarditis (inflammation around the heart), but it didn't quite fit the criteria, and the patient was having worrisome chest pain. The other, more sinister possibility was that the patient was having a massive heart attack occluding almost all coronary vessels.

"Your job," said Dr. Loud, "is to keep paging the cardiologist until he answers."

This sounded familiar, but I didn't see how my 3 a.m. pages were so different from her 3 a.m. pages. Fortunately, on my second try, the cardiologist picked up and said, "Why are you calling my children's telephone line? I never answer this one."

I explained and faxed him the EKG.

After I hung up, Dr. Loud showed me the latest cardiogram. The ST changes had settled down.

"So it is cardiac," I told Dr. Loud. She nodded, and we both understood that this was a temporary reprieve as well as a diagnosis.

I was processing another, non-medical revelation: Dr. Loud was scared.

All that noise, all that bluster, even the broken ribs, and she was terrified that the pregnant patient might bleed out or the man in resus might code any second.

Anger, or aversion, is really about fear.

How angry was I?

I never considered suing the obstetrician about Isadora. I turned the anger on myself. I didn't want to look in the mirror. I'd hated gaining weight and developing a little belly, yet now I hated losing the belly and fitting back in my old clothes.

Other pregnant women still made me grit my teeth.

I even asked my husband, "Why couldn't our dog have died instead?" I loved our dog, but I loved our baby more.

Yep. I knew aversion.

I called my friend Isabel and listed my many infractions: when my husband and I went to Costa Rica, I didn't realize I was pregnant, so I didn't bring folic acid and was too cheap to buy more; I took a dip in the hot and cold therapeutic pools; I'd given myself the flu shot when I was unwittingly six weeks along; I got my cavities done at eleven weeks.

"Melissa," she said, "some women do cocaine when they're pregnant, and you're worried about going to the dentist?"

I paused. "It was the carelessness of it. I wasn't worried about her when I did it."

"Okay," she said.

But she did make me think. In one of my favourite children's books, *A Summer to Die*, a wise friend says, "Sometimes it's nice to have someone to blame, even if it's only yourself."

The problem was, once I stopped blaming and hating myself, Isadora would be one step closer to gone.

Lust

Sensual Desire

Do I want stuff?
   OMG.
   I looooove stuff.
   But I was raised by cheap Chinese immigrants, so my craving takes the form of obsession for tiny, peculiar things, like a $10 robot watch I must buy on eBay stat. I also love to eat.
   This is usually a great distraction. But when we buried Isadora's ashes in our backyard, it stopped working. It started seeming cheap and unimportant.
   Sylvia Boorstein made the point that desire is normal for everyone, even ultra-nuns, but if you get stuck craving the one thing you cannot have, that's creating suffering.
   Matt kept busy. He built her a little box out of purpleheart wood. He tried to dig her grave, even though the ground was frozen. It kept him busy.
   I didn't want anything—except another baby.
   That, I wanted really badly.
   That, I could not stop thinking about.
   I borrowed *Taking Charge of Your Fertility* from the library. I went on the message boards. I initiated sex and really did try to stand on my head afterward, or at least did a shoulderstand.
   It distracted me more than a little.
   But I was still in mourning.

Restlessness

Worry or Remorse

"When I can't sleep," said my grandmother, "I look at my pictures and I feel better." She pointed at a photo of the sweaters she'd knit.

I nodded. Even before emergency room shifts screwed up my sleep, I was a crummy sleeper. If anything went the slightest bit wrong in my life, I'd wake up at 3 a.m., mulling it over and over again. My mother wakes up at 3 or 4 a.m. regularly in order to cook or generally "get things done" before she crashes at 7 a.m.

Sylvia Boorstein calls this fretting. And she points out that you feel like you're doing something because you devote so much energy to it, even if it's just wringing your hands.

I can major in worry any day of the week. I can create sound and fury on a dime.

Occasionally, it helps. I can brainstorm like nobody's business and generate unusual solutions.

But no amount of worrying was going to bring Isadora back. And in fact, everyone kept telling me that worrying could interfere with conceiving another baby, so in effect, I should worry about worrying.

So what else was I supposed to do? Just sit here, helpless, with my torment?

Really?

Doubt

I called up my friends, rotating through them so as not to exhaust them with my angst.

They knew doubt, too. A friend's uncle had died on a trip overseas, and he felt guilty about that.

"How could you have helped him?" I asked.

"I was thinking of going with him. He could have told me earlier if he'd had chest pain. And I could have resuscitated him on the plane."

When you're a doctor and your job is to save lives, you get to the point that any death, any illness, feels like something you could have prevented. Did your mother develop diabetes? Well, gosh darn it, you should have dragged her on a walk every day and lectured her not to put jam on her toast. You knew the data on preventative medicine. So why didn't you do it?

Having some power and some control makes you think that you should be able to control everything. Therefore everything that goes wrong is your fault.

My husband is an engineer and an atheist. He believes in facts, not doubt. Thus, he is an excellent sleeper.

"Do you think about Isadora?" I asked him.

"Sometimes. When I'm driving."

"Do you worry about her?"

"No." He touched my hair. "She's not hurting anymore."

But how could we be sure? What if our baby went to hell? What if she was reincarnated as an ant that got squished? My doubt not only covered this life, but the next.

I asked my Hindu friend, who assured me that Isadora was not a bug, "because she didn't do anything wrong."

Another friend, who was a Christian, told me, "I think she has her own soul."

My atheist friend Leah said, "I don't think you would see her again, but you could encounter her molecules again. That bit of carbon, or that piece of oxygen ... " This didn't help.

I drew a little comfort from grilling religious and non-religious people about their views of the afterlife.

I read one line in a book, "Let go and let God." I'd probably heard it before and ignored it, but something inside me released when I read it this time. I realized that if I could abdicate responsibility, if I could say and believe, *I did not have control over this. I'm not responsible. Some higher power's got to take the hit on this one, I would feel better.*

George W. Bush struck me as a happy guy. He did whatever he felt like. Make up evidence about weapons of mass destruction? Sure. Spy on your own people? Why not? Keep a baseball score card of all the "enemies" you killed? Right on! Everything was hunky-dory because Jesus had chosen him to lead "the free world."

He never had doubt.

Now, that was why Kurt Vonnegut labeled him a psychopath, so I couldn't go there.

But in general, setting aside my doubt and trusting in a higher power? That would really help me relax.

I just couldn't do it.

Sloth and Torpor

When I was a kid, my mother used to yank the blanket off of me every day of summer vacation and yell, "What are you going to *do* today?"

I'd growl, "I want to sleep."

She would goggle at me and say, "I've been up since 3 a.m.!"

"So?" I'd grumble, but of course, she'd already woken me up, so I'd get dressed and start accomplishing things, as she intended. They kept me in summer school, camp, organ lessons, swim classes, and gymnastics lessons, so it wasn't like I had a whole lot of days to sleep in anyway.

When our family moved to Germany for over two years, I grew to loathe traveling. Not only was I an annoying 10-year-old who wanted to stay at home, read, and, at absolute maximum, go to McDonald's, but my family's brand of travel was to pick a country, drive for days, sleep in the car, and buy things, filling up the trunk and all the leg space. We'd brush our teeth in restaurant bathrooms and rent a hotel every week or so for a shower. When it was time to sleep, my parents would recline their seats in luxury. My brother and I slumped in the backseat, leaning on our respective windows or on the headrest between us as we struggled to sleep sitting up.

By the time I got to high school, I was surprised to call a friend at 10 a.m. and have her mother answer, "I'm sorry, she's sleeping. May I take a message?"

I was highly impressed. My mother would have salivated at the opportunity to bang on my door and wake me up. *You have to get up! Your friend is calling!*

Needless to say, I don't "get" sloth or torpor.

I see it all the time, though. Patients are always asking me for work notes. I'm like, *Why?* And they're like, *My nose is dripping.*

I stare at them with the same kind of incomprehension as my mother, who boycotted summer vacations.

Meanwhile, my husband is very good at sloth. I took the first enjoyable vacation of my life with him, a casual road trip to the Maritimes. Yes, I had a guide book, and I booked where we'd sleep and (more importantly) chose where we'd eat. But we didn't have to study up on the history. We didn't have to tear from one "must see" sight to the next.

One of my neighbours suggested we go on vacation after Isadora died.

I considered a conference in New Orleans, during its famous jazz festival. But it felt like we were celebrating Isadora's death. I couldn't do it.

On the other hand, we'd already booked a trip to Hawaii in autumn, with our air miles, before I got pregnant. I didn't cancel it.

My neighbour put me in touch with a minister whom I'll call Eleanor. She asked me, "Are you being gentle with yourself?"

That stopped me cold.

I had to say, "No."

I thought, *Why would I be gentle with myself?*

I didn't want to be gentle with myself. I wanted my baby. And if I couldn't take care of her physical body, well by gum, I was starting on this path to look after her spiritual life.

The fact that the minister had asked me this question gave me pause.

Should I be gentle with myself? Was that what people did?

In one book, a mother of twins who'd died said that she used to send weekly flowers to their graves, but then she started sending them to herself every Monday, so that she'd remember them.

What a cow, I thought. *Sending herself flowers! The nerve! What about her babies? They're the ones who deserve flowers.*

It was like these people were speaking a foreign language. I listened to them carefully and pondered their words afterwards, trying to decipher their meaning, but I still didn't get it.

Custom Pop Quiz

Your baby died. You:

a) sue the obstetrician. Someone's gotta pay.

b) dream about the baby you must have. Not to replace the one who died. Of course not. But you have so much love to give. You already have the nursery set up. And it wouldn't hurt to buy a teddy bear, right? Just one little bear? How about a stroller? You have nephews who visit who could use a stroller.

c) go back to work. Hit the gym. Keep busy. But your mind is going 1000 miles per hour.

d) worry about what you did wrong. Was it because you forgot your folic acid?

e) lie in bed. You need your rest.

Stress Test

Charlotte Joko Beck wrote in *Nothing Special: Living Zen* that you should observe your response to stress. Not to judge it in any way, but take a look.

Just like stress is different for different people, our responses are all different.

Another spiritual thinker called Gurdjieff said our response to pressure was our "chief feature."

Okay.

Fine.

I started observing. Of course, it was much easier to remember how other people responded to stress, and how I responded to that.

Do you avoid stress?

That's my husband. Don't say anything, don't make a scene, just leave. When we were on family vacation in a condo in Hawaii, my parents started making bone soup, which means hours of simmering bones on the stovetop, stinking up the place, in order to make tasteless, greasy water.

"Matthew! I made you bone soup!" trilled my mother.

I looked at Matt. He gave me a look back, but didn't say anything.

"He doesn't want it, Mom," I called back.

"Matthew! Come and get your bone soup!"

Matt stayed sitting on the balcony with me.

"Mom, he's not going to eat it," I said.

"Matthew! Melissa! Come and get it!"

"I'm not going to eat it, Mom," I said, coming into the kitchen.

"Whaaaaat? You're not going to eat bone soup?" she repeated, incredulous, as if I hadn't stopped eating bone soup five years before.

"No, Mom. I never eat bone soup."

"Well, fine. Dad, do you want another bowl?"

My father said, "Sure." He sucked it down.

Meanwhile, my mother made a special delivery of bone soup to the balcony and placed it on the folding table in front of Matt.

Half an hour later, we were packing up to leave the condo, and I asked Matt, "Did you eat it?"

"Of course not."

"Well, where is it?"

"On the balcony."

"But you can't leave it out there. The cleaners will find it and charge us a cleaning fee." I stuck my head out of the room and said, "Mom, you'd better eat the soup that's on the balcony."

"No, that's Matthew's!"

"He won't eat it," I said.

"Whaaaaat? He's not going to eat bone soup?"

I wasn't sure how to classify my mother's response to stress. Denial, probably.

Do you try to act like a star?

Yes, ma'am. That was me. If someone criticized me, I'd bite back my fury before I tried ever-harder to reach whatever goal they wanted from me. If they said, "You should've studied for sixteen hours straight," I'd aim for seventeen while still striving to sing, dance, learn how to do the splits, and give my husband a blow job at the same time.

Now that life had cut my heart out, though, I was going to have to come up with a new response to stress. Death doesn't care about your straight A's or how shiny your hair is. Unfortunately.

Do you get angry?

Oh, yeah.

I'm good at fighting. I didn't cry in front of nearly any of the doctors, until the last moments, when I was delivering Isadora and would never get her back. I made an effort to sit up for my vitals. I asked for, and received, the medications I wanted, and decreased my vital sign monitoring so that nurses didn't have to wake me up to take my blood pressure at 2 a.m.

The hospital gave me a structure to fight against. I knew what to do then.

I know how to be angry. I know how to write petitions. I know how to kick up a fuss and tell people to go to hell.

But this. This emptiness. This uncertainty. This moral morass of no right answers and no easy solutions. It was fighting the tofu, as the writer Natalie Goldberg said.

I didn't know how to do that.

Three Poisons

Luckily, the Buddha had already taken a look at our stress responses and slotted them into three categories: passion, aversion, or indifference.

Pema Chödrön explained this really well in her book, *Start Where You Are*.

For example, how do you feel about chocolate?

Could you rhapsodize about the finest Criollo cocoa beans on www.gimmeechocolaterightnow.com?

Passion.

Do you lecture people about the evils of fat, sugary cocoa butter because you would never let it touch your virgin mouth?

Aversion.

Are you part of the 0.00001 percent of the population who doesn't think much about chocolate, one way or another?

Indifference.

Passion. Aversion. Indifference.

One chocolate bar. Three different reactions.

You could take a time machine to the Hanging Gardens of Babylon, but if you can hardly see the palm trees because you're missing your smart phone so bad, that's passion. If you bumped your shoulder when you landed in the garden, and you keep yelling about it so loudly that you're shaking the stone columns, that's aversion. And if you just look at your watch because, Seven Wonders of the World, whatever, that's ancient history, man ... welcome to indifference.

If I looked at my life, I could easily see how passion and aversion had ruled my life up until now.

The great thing about Buddhism is the lack of judgement. Pema Chödrön called her chapter on the topic "Poison as Medicine." She pointed out the good stuff about the three poisons.

Passion is fun. Who hasn't made friends because you're both crazy about someone else no one else understands, like origami wig-makers? One friend said she broke up with a boyfriend after seven years because they were so mismatched when it came to trying new things. He always had to eat the same food, preferably at home, with the same friends and family, whereas she loved to explore new foods and new cultures. "I made him a curry, and he made this face, like it was poison, and he actually started to heave!"

But what if you are shacking up with your "soul mate" while wifey's bringing up your five kids? Or you bankrupt yourself buying the contents of the Buck4U store to foist bucketloads of plastic back-scratchers on unsuspecting relatives? Extreme passion is not cool.

Aversion gave me energy. I could push my way through a 14-hour night shift and the drive home if I were pissed off enough. But anger got dangerous when I found myself plugging into people. Like, say, other pregnant women.

As for indifference ... well, my husband could teach me about indifference. For example, he didn't care much about food in general. "Fuel," he said. He had also uttered such heresies as "I could just eat out of a freezer for the rest of my life," and "I wish I could take a pill so I wouldn't have to bother eating."

Sacrilege, man.

On the other hand, I could see that I spend a lot of time thinking about food. Worrying about the empty fridge. Getting stressed if I ran out of goodies during a busy shift. Hurrying out the door to buy local, organic food from farmers' markets and carving out the time to do something besides toss the wilted lettuce.

If I could stop craving food so much, I could relax slightly. So indifference could be a bit of medicine for me, just like sloth.

Indifference occasionally came to my rescue after Isadora died, when my brain shut down. I read a few condolences on my e-mail and I thought, *That didn't happen to me. Why are they writing to me about it?* My friend Beatrice said that she and her mom wept over the idea of a tiny coffin. My first thought was, *I don't need a coffin.*

The denial felt tolerable for the two seconds that it lasted.

So indifference could be a useful time and energy saver.

But it also drained the pleasure out of life. Pema Chödrön compared it to sitting in front of the Grand Canyon with a paper bag over your head.

Passion, aversion, and indifference. Each could bring you pleasure, poison, or both.

Thanks for pointing that out, Buddha.

Blame (The BMW Story)

Imagine you're driving your brand new BMW. You're a doctor, so you're programmed to want a BMW, and you worked hard for it. One day, you're leaving the hospital, and a minivan rolls backward, about to T-bone your precious vehicle on the passenger side.

You honk. You yell.

The van keeps rolling.

You can't back up or advance because other cars have pulled up tight around you.

Crunch.

Your passenger door caves in. The van stops.

a) Through the van's tinted windows, you now see that there's no one inside. The brakes must have failed. How strange. Oh, well, time to make an insurance claim.

b) The van's door pops open. The driver's already yelling, "Sorry! I didn't see you!"

Charlotte Joko Beck told this story in her excellent book, *Nothing Special: Living Zen*, except she used rowboats instead of cars in her example. She pointed out that if no one was there to blame, you'd just repaint your rowboat, but if you had someone to blame, hoo boy. Start shouting, stamping your feet, calling on cell phones, activating lawyers, and initiating flame wars now.

Actually, doctors and nurses might not. We know what matters, since every day, we see sick and dying people. We might not sweat the small stuff—unless we're burned out and furious, in which case, step aside.

I didn't blame anyone else for Isadora's death. Even so, I had trouble reconciling myself to an empty van or rowboat.

I already knew that bad things happened to good people. I saw it every day. We liked to talk about risk factors, especially modifiable ones, which basically means that we can blame you for them (smoking, obesity, even aging seems like something lame that ought to happen to other people). But it's very unsatisfying to have no one to sue. It means that all you can do is accept.

I didn't want to do that.

Forbidden Happiness

I was afraid to be happy.

I wrote, *"It stabs my heart. Who do you think you are?* How dare you be happy without your daughter?"

I still couldn't believe what happened. *We have to start over again? I'm not pregnant anymore? I can't get my daughter back?*

All my plans—stop the night shifts, enjoy a summer with my new baby, wear maternity bras, buy the great car seat, and settle the stroller debates—erased. My firstborn, deleted, and no one except me felt like a single, endless scream.

And when could we have another baby? I initially took comfort that other people had borne children after tragedy. But every day without conceiving another baby felt like a private form of torture, like someone was applying electroshocks to my genitals, but I had to keep on smiling as if it felt just grand.

If we did conceive and were lucky enough to carry a baby to term, that would take another nine months, and then I'd have to worry about Sudden infant death syndrome.

My friend Beatrice didn't want me to wait that long to be happy. She asked me not to forget "the amazing person you've made yourself into."

Should I cut short my maternity leave and force myself back to work, even though my insides cringed at the thought? My cousin Karen pointed out that putting pressure on myself made me crazy.

I was so afraid of being nothing.

In the mornings, I could still laugh a little or have a sense of purpose. But I totally crashed at night, and at various points during the day.

Which my friend Maggie said was normal.

One day, I realized that I didn't want to kill myself. I considered that progress. I could see infant steps of progress in my grief.

But I was scared to be happy without Isadora.

I still laughed on the phone with my friends. Matt forced me to laugh with silly faces and jokes. For some reason, that was okay. But the pure joy of being outdoors, of watching my dog and my husband at play, of me talking to our dog, Olo, in my little voice, the same voice I'd used for my baby—that was verboten. My heart seized up. My self-loathing demanded justice. *You bitch. Your daughter is dead. How dare you?*

I woke up at 5 a.m. It was too cloudy to see the stars. The moon was just a dim yellow haze. And I thought, clearly, *Isadora doesn't want you to be depressed.*

I knew this. I knew it with rock hard certainty. The brave part of me, the Melissa-I-used-to-be, spoke the truth.

Then the same hard voice continued, *But maybe your husband would be better off without all your grief.*

I could see the point. I had been a burden ever since we came home from the hospital. And I despised myself for it. Even though I knew I'd supported him plenty of times. Even though I knew he loved me.

I was a drag. That was the plain truth, too.

So I poked him awake and asked if he'd be better off without me.

"*No,*" he groaned. "But I wish you wouldn't steal the blankets."

I hadn't been sleeping well for the past few hours, so I knew hadn't been doing my usual unconscious blanket theft. "I haven't been."

"Not now," he agreed, still half-asleep.

I was sick of myself. Sick of this self-punishment.

If I could turn on the Buddhism, I'd call all of this "fear" and "aversion" and walk away from it.

I seemed to be stuck right in the middle of it.

All I knew was that I had to keep on going.

Yoga

I finally realized that there was one path toward meditation that usually worked for me, and I'd been doing it for almost a decade.

Back in university, one of my friends had said, "I'm taking yoga."

"What's that like?" I asked, curious. This was before yoga studios were as ubiquitous as sandwich shops.

"It's wonderful. Before this, I couldn't even touch my toes."

"And now you can?" I asked.

"Now, I can."

We were barely 22 years old, but I was getting stiffer, too, probably from sitting and studying so much. I signed up.

From the beginning, I dreaded some of the poses. Why did we have to do downward dog all the time? How come my leg twinged during triangle pose? And forget wheel/upward bow, where I was supposed to lie on my back, plant my hands and feet on the ground, and push my hips up and my head back, making my body into an arch top bridge. I couldn't do that when I was five years old, and I couldn't do it now, either.

I kept stealing glances at the other students. Well, let's be honest, I competed with them. It seemed mightily unfair that one woman who looked about twice my age could touch her toes better than I could.

But after a while, I was able to concentrate on my own poses and ignore the other people's contortions. I closed my eyes, which helped.

The teacher kept encouraging us to breathe audibly. I'd unconsciously learned to make almost no sound while I exhaled. I had to learn how to breathe again.

At the end, the teacher lit incense, and we lay on our backs in *Savasana,* which is Sanskrit for corpse pose, more delicately called "final relaxation pose." The teacher read a poem. I almost fell asleep, or at least into a pleasant state where I didn't have to run screaming from item to item on my to-do list.

I was sort of, kind of ... meditating.

And when I left, I felt so much better. Relaxed. Happier. Noticing stuff without getting wrought up about it.

"Blissed out," was how one of the other students put it.

I kept doing yoga on and off, ever since.

For the first twenty minutes of yoga class, I'd be fighting it. *I don't like this class. The teacher is annoying. I want to work on my hamstrings. Are we going to do any backbends?*

If I was practicing at home, it was worse, because I could literally click on hundreds of different classes on yogatoday.com and never do more than three minutes of each. Or I could be writing, studying, washing dishes, or paying the bills—dozens of tasks that pulled me away from yoga. So sometimes, I needed to just get out to the studio and surrender.

But no matter where I was, if I could get past the first twenty or especially forty minutes, I could just keep going with the flow. I could actually lie down afterward and meditate.

The first yoga class I attended after Isadora died, I cried.

Meditation 2.0

A stem cell researcher named Doris Taylor took blood samples from a man before and after fifteen minutes of meditation and noticed a "huge" upsurge in positive stem cells. That was a sample size of one, but it did show a concrete way to measure meditation's restorative powers.

I liked Martha Beck's meditation strategies in *The Joy Diet*. She said that if you really couldn't sit still, then you should get moving. Do something mindless that gets your heart pumping, like running or blading. Even before I read her book, I was out skiing with my dog every day.

She also suggested the opposite strategy, if you were bereft of energy. Lie down and look at something, like a candle flame.

I liked that. I could build a fire in our wood stove and sit for minutes, hypnotized by flames and basking in the warmth. Back in the day, I used to enjoy staring at candle flames and playing with the wax.

Other stare-worthy things she mentioned were the ocean's surf, a river, or a wheat field blowing in the wind.

The last one reminded me of the uncle in Joy Kogawa's book, *Obasan*. His waterfront property had been seized by the Canadian government because of his Japanese heritage. They sent him and his family to slave in Alberta. He never made it back to British Columbia, but he used to sit in the wheat fields and watch the wheat bend in the wind. It reminded him of the ocean.

That might seem like an irrelevant story, but *Obasan* was a beautiful yet painful book, and this story is the sort of thing that can come up during meditation.

I meditated enough, in my half-hearted way, that I might have figured out the point of meditation: there was nothing else to do except think.

And when you thought, you remembered all sorts of stuff, including stuff that made you feel ashamed, but you couldn't even get up and call the person to apologize, because you were meditating, so you had to keep sitting there with your shame and worry and anger.

Eventually, you separated yourself from your thoughts, from your painful past and your plans for the future. You were just kinda there.

Present.

Someone asked Buddha, "Who do you think you are?"

He answered, "I am the Awake."

As far as I could tell, all that meant is, he was fully present. And he told everyone about it so that we could aim for that, too.

Does that sound too new-age-y? Alice Morse Earle's quote has become a classic: "Yesterday is history. Tomorrow is a mystery. Today is a gift. That's why it is called the present."

Today did not seem like such a present. But I knew what they meant.

Dedication

In her book *How Not to Be Afraid of Your Own Life*, Susan Piver said you should finish off your meditation with a "dedication of merit." That is, you should direct whatever goodness came out of your meditation to the benefit of all beings, including yourself.

This was not such a foreign concept to me. In yoga class, teachers might ask you to dedicate that hour of practice to someone or something you love. "Every time you bring your hands together in *namaste* (pressing your palms together in front of your chest), bring yourself back to that dedication."

You could wish for world peace or inner peace or whatever you wanted.

The Buddhist teacher Sakyong Mipham Rinpoche said that if you don't do the dedication of merit at the end of your meditation, it's like not pressing the save button before you shut down your computer. Meditation benefits you more if think of others as well as yourself.

I vacillated. Most of the time, I'd pray and pray for Isadora, but I'd quickly slip in a wish for future babies. And once I happened to think of our dog Olo's cheerful, furry face.

It never occurred to me to concentrate on the people around me until a yoga teacher said, "If you have extra energy, give it to the other people in the room. If you need energy, take it in from the room." Suddenly, instead of competing with the people surrounding me, I felt kindly toward them. We were helping each other.

Then I started worrying about Isadora again.

Labels

The more I reflected on my thoughts, the more I realized how viciously I spoke to myself.

I e-mailed an online friend who was also desperately trying to conceive. "I'm the one holding the gun to my head every month. No one else is clicking the stopwatch and saying, 'Are you pregnant yet? You barren mare! You horrendous loser!' Sure, other people might wonder, but they're mostly interested in their own lives. They're not thinking these bad things. We are."

In *Zen and the Art of Eating*, Ronna Kabatznick wrote that we really get attached to labels. "I am a vegetarian." "I am thin." "I am fit." Then we try super hard to keep those labels accurate, by dieting and exercising and eating only organic quinoa and goji berries.

I'd been addicted to those labels and the satisfaction I got from them. I wrote, *I realize that I value myself conditionally: because I am a doctor. Because I am a writer. Because I am thin. Because I am a mother. Because I did something environmentally friendly.*

But it's garbage. Because when those labels fall apart, I castigate myself. "You're not a mother. You lost your daughter. You're not working, so you're no longer a doctor. You're a fat bitch and everyone hates you."

Those labels had been ripped away. I was in freefall. What should I do now?

Part II

Loving-Kindness and Community

The Mustard Seed *Sangha*

> What you are is what you have been;
> what you will be is what you do now.
> —Buddha

Mustard Seeds

Kisa Gotami's child died.

She couldn't believe it. She thought the child was very ill, not dead. She carried the little body on her shoulder, asking everyone for a cure.

Finally, a man told her, "Your child has died, but before I do anything for your little one, I would like you to collect some mustard seeds from a home where nobody has ever died."

The task seemed straightforward. With great hope, she set off from house to house. Every home offered her mustard seeds, but she couldn't accept them, because each family had endured death at some point.

Eventually, she understood that everyone has a loved one who dies. She understood the depths of her own pain and her own grief. She realized that she had been carrying around her child's corpse.

Kisa Gotami buried her child and returned to the wise man, to learn more from him. In time, she became a nun and attained enlightenment.

The wise man, born as Siddhartha Gautama, became known as the Buddha.

I was not alone.

I was scared and sad, but I was not alone. I was surrounded by people whose mustard seeds had been bathed in grief.

First of all, I had Matt. We'd been together since high school. He'd always stood by me. Part of me worried that I'd lose him, too. Not in the cheatin', lyin' bastard way, but in the "he drives to Montreal every day, dodging psychos in three lanes of traffic, while poorly maintained overpasses could collapse around him" kind of way.

I couldn't bear to lose Matt, to sustain a tragedy on top of this tragedy. I wrote, "It would be like walking down the street and someone tearing my lungs out and saying, 'Okay, you didn't need these anyway, right?'"

Matt had cried, too.

He cried just after I delivered Isadora. He cradled her tiny body in his hands and walked over to the window, so the sunlight would fall on her face.

He cried a second time the next morning, when they brought her up to say goodbye, and her miniature body was stiff with cold.

But mostly, he didn't cry, and he didn't say a whole lot. He picked out a spot for her ashes in our back yard, between two maple trees. He tried to dig her a grave, even though the February ground was frozen solid. He made a box for her ashes out of purpleheart wood.

"Men grieve differently," people of both sexes told me repeatedly. If the women said it, their tone implied that men didn't grieve as well.

Actually, I thought Matt's way looked a lot better than mine. He could still sleep. He didn't seem to be screaming endlessly inside. But two friends told me to watch out for him. "Sometimes the silent ones carry things deep inside themselves."

We held a ceremony for Isadora. It helped immeasurably to be surrounded by people who loved us and who grieved with us. Some of our friends drove from the other side of the province to be with us. My brother made it even though the Queensway, Ottawa's main highway, closed down.

We read a few passages aloud, not from any religious tradition, but quotes I'd picked from Sark, Barbara Kingsolver, and a children's book called *Little Bug*.

Matt and his friend Balaji played two songs on the guitar. One song was called "Lament" and the other was "Tears in the Rain."

But it wasn't all weeping. We fussed over Olo the wonder dog. My dad served food and drinks. My mother said, "You look good!"

I told Matt afterward, "I don't want to look good. I want to have my daughter."

"You can look good, and it will help you make another daughter." He waggled his eyebrows at me, earning a small laugh.

My cousin Karen couldn't come, but she promised to call me every day. That became my lifeline when my other friends' calls started to peter out after a month or so. She pointed out some useful things, like that I seemed better in the mornings. I said, "I feel one hundred percent better after talking to you!" She answered, "Good. But don't feel bad if you crash in two hours." Which was exactly what happened.

Openness *(Bodhichitta)*

There's a line in *Taking Charge of Your Fertility* like, "Deciding to have a child ... means wearing your heart outside your body for the rest of your life."

Yes. I understood. It was that powerful and that painful.

In my own way, I was carrying Isadora's little body around, asking for help.

Following other people's advice, I dragged Matt to two bereavement group meetings. One woman said, "I've lost other family members. It was like losing a leg or an arm. But losing my child was like losing my heart."

I knew exactly what she meant.

And yet I was still alive. Technically, my heart still beat in my chest. I wrote afterward, "What does that mean? Isadora wasn't really my heart? Or she was, but it was like a bad heart attack, and now I have a lot of scar tissue, and my ejection fraction is only 20 percent, but I can still walk and talk, albeit not as easily as I used to?" (For the non-medical types, I will translate this as, "How can I be alive when she's not?")

I wanted to be with Isadora. Suicide crossed my mind, but I yearned desperately for another baby. Since I was highly trained as a doctor and all, I knew that my death was not compatible with conception.

There was only one upside to this hurtin'. Rumi and other Sufi masters said, "A broken heart is an open heart."

Buddhists call this softness, this kind of openness, *bodhichitta*.

Bodhichitta is a Sanskrit word. *Chitta* means "mind" as well as "heart" or "perspective." *Bodhi* means "awakened," "enlightened," or "fully open."

In *Things Fall Apart*, Pema Chödrön explained that *bodhichitta* lives inside of everyone, just like butter is contained inside milk. Everyone's got *bodhichitta*. Vicious serial killer or grandmother, politician or newborn baby, Wall Street shark or great white shark. Everybody's got a soft spot.

Trungpa Rinpoche put it like this: "Everyone loves something, even if it's only tortillas."

When Pema Chödrön explained the concept in her book, *The Places That Scare You*, she called *bodhichitta* an open wound.

I knew that normal people opened up after having children. "I couldn't watch the news after my daughter was born," said my friend, Leah. "It bothered me so much."

Having a baby and then losing her broke me open. It connected me with the rest of humanity, the rest of life. But it hurt so much, too.

Everything ached.

The day after I delivered her, we crashed at my brother's house, since our house in the country was too far away. I woke up sobbing, but let Matt go back to sleep so I could apologize to my brother about an incident in high school: my parents had grounded Brian on New Year's Eve, and I'd been secretly glad because I hadn't been invited to any parties, and now he'd have to stay home with me.

Brian hugged me now and kissed my hair. He said he remembered that New Year's, but it didn't matter—I was a great sister and shouldn't worry.

It helped a little.

I knew that I hadn't done anything that New Year's Eve. Still, I felt guilty about everything. I wrote, "It's like Isadora opened up my skin and makes me feel all the things I'd buried."

To be perfectly honest, I think the trick is to *bodhichitta* is to let yourself crack open without cracking up. Months later, I managed to snag a local family doctor even though she was no longer accepting patients. She was the only doctor who asked me for Isadora's name and wrote it in my chart. Then she asked, "Did you drink or take drugs?"

I laughed. "No." It hadn't even occurred to me.

She just looked at me. "I knew a couple who lost their child. They were drunk for a year."

Another doctor who'd suffered a full-term stillbirth told me, "I went to one grief group. One couple had lost their child two years ago, and I was better off than they were."

You don't get any prizes for mourning the most efficiently. There is no "best." But I couldn't relate to people mired in their own mudpools. I couldn't really help them. And I didn't always connect with their ways of helping me.

"Don't worry, your daughter's an angel now." (How would you know? What is an angel, anyway?)

"They make special jewelry that you can put her ashes in." (No, thanks.)

I did thank the bereavement group for a gold butterfly pin, which I pinned to the collar of my red fleece jacket. And I liked their idea of pasting stickers into our Christmas cards to represent Isadora so that even if I didn't sign her name, she would be represented in my heart and in my mind.

But one of bereavement people called me afterward to say, "I would fight for my daughter. If God came down and said only one of us could have her daughter back, I would fight you tooth and nail."

That was so bizarre, I never went back to the bereavement meetings. I figured I would machete my own path through the wilderness, *bodhichitta* and all.

Bodhichitta is the only thing that is supposed to heal difficult times.

But it hurts.

It throbs.

Pir-o-Murshid Inayat Khan, another Sufi teacher, wrote, "Out of the shell of the broken heart arises the newborn soul."

Got Nectar?

A flower that is full of nectar does not have to beg the honey-bees to pollinate it.
—Sri Lankan saying quoted by Bhante Y. Wimala

This saying made me think of pregnancy.
Well, everything made me think about pregnancy. Lost babies, inability to get pregnant ... my mind kept going there. Was I still full of nectar, even though my womb was empty? Would I get "pollinated"?
Bhante, a monk, went on to explain that a flower may appear beautiful, but if it doesn't have much nectar, the bees might buzz around it but won't linger.
I wanted to argue with Bhante that scientists have shown that flowers do sort of beg for pollination. If you look at flowers under ultraviolet light, they've evolved elaborate patterns to entice bees.
But I understood his point. He was basically telling me to keep it real.
Now that my life had just been eviscerated, I realized just how unreal a lot of it had been.
For example, I'd worried a lot about medicine and how to best treat patients, but also about my preceptors' evaluations and how many patients I could see per hour.
I also worried about embarrassingly superficial things like if I could wear my skinniest pants.
My husband hated when I complained about my weight. At one point, he announced that he wasn't going to answer any

more questions on that score, except to say, "ARGH!" Beatrice, my best friend from high school, told me that I was a stick and had body dysmorphic disorder. I just laughed at them.

My fear of fat continued during pregnancy. At sixteen weeks along, I developed a little potbelly. I felt terribly self-conscious about it. I wanted to wear a sign around my neck that said, *I'm not fat, I'm pregnant!* But since we weren't telling anyone, I felt beefy.

After we lost Isadora, I hated myself for worrying about my weight. I wished I'd enjoyed being pregnant.

Now, I was in the worst of all worlds. My baby was dead and I was still fat.

One month to the day after Isadora died, I could fit back into my skinniest jeans. I looked in the mirror and thought, *Big deal.*

The problem hadn't been my weight. It had been my head. And that was a lot harder to fix that than to lose a few pounds.

I realized that for me, weight was a socially acceptable thing to worry about. Easy to fixate on. Easy to find someone to moan along with me. But for my entire life, I'd felt ten pounds heavier than I actually was.

I needed to move past that. Because really, it wasn't important.

What was important? Respecting Isadora's life. Finding meaning in her short existence. Reassuring myself that even if I could no longer see her or touch her, she was at peace.

And somehow, eventually, finding a little peace for myself.

I needed to stop feeling okay only when I met the most stringent set of guidelines, i.e. doctor/mother/writer/wife who saves lives while fitting into the tiniest miniskirt.

The bees know better.

I had to rebuild my life. I had to construct new dreams.

I had to start thinking about nectar and less about appearance.

All Mustard Seeds Are One

"You sound down," said a friend, over the phone. We had gone through undergrad together, and now he was doing his post-doctorate work. He was a few years older than me and already had a few kids. I looked to him for advice sometimes, but we usually kept it light.

I shrugged. "What do you expect? My baby's dead."

"Whoa, do you have to put it that way?"

"Well, what other way do you expect me to put it?"

"You lost a pregnancy, not a baby—"

"I'm going to stop you right there," I said. "This has never happened to you, and you don't know what it's like. Let's talk about something else."

I wasn't angry at him. For no good reason, I tended to give guys a free pass more than my female friends. But I also subconsciously moved him to my "do not call" list.

He was a nice guy, but he didn't get it. I had to find my own posse of people who understood.

Wait. After I hung up the phone, I realized that I had accomplished something.

One of my greatest fears was that someone would tell me I was not a mother. That Isadora didn't "count." That she wasn't a real baby and nobody cared about her.

But when this guy did exactly that ("a pregnancy, not a baby"), I told him off and moved on.

I defended us.

I didn't need his permission to call her a baby.

I didn't let it get me down that he wouldn't call her one.

I got nectar.

However, the more I talked to other people grappling with grief, the more I heard "It's not the same."

I'd already noted the classic "Men mourn differently. It's not the same."

But some other top of the pops from other mourners included:

"Losing a child is completely different from losing another family member. It's not the same."

"It's different, losing a baby compared to losing an adult child. It's not the same."

"She compared it to putting up a child for adoption! It's not the same."

"I've had a miscarriage and I had a stillbirth. It's not the same."

I knew where they were coming from. Honestly, when other people said, "I'm so sad that my 103-year-old grandmother died. She had so much left to live for! I know exactly what you're going through!", I would think to myself, *You do?*

But then I realized what they were really saying, which was, *I feel you. You're not alone.*

I could live with that.

I thought all this "You're not the same" or "You don't understand" was a waste of energy. Aversion, actually.

Yes, I agreed that losing a baby was different, and I liked to go online and talk to people who understood. I related more to people who'd lost babies of the same age, under the same circumstances. But overall, I thought that grief was grief. If you had lost someone or something and you really felt it, if you were bowled over instead of brushing it off and pretending everything was fine, then you were my people.

When mourners argued and divided and parsed and separated grief like this, it reminded me of a joke that my husband once told me. I couldn't remember the exact details, but it went kind of like,

"Hey! I'm a Deist."

"Me too."

"Traditional Deist or Secular Deist?"

"Traditional."

"Me too. Traditional Eastern Orthodox or Traditional Western Covenant?"

"Traditional Eastern Orthodox."

"Me too. Traditional Eastern Orthodox from before or after the 1888 reformation?"

"Before."

"Heretic!" (Person A pushes person B off of a cliff.)

What I liked about Buddhism was its inclusiveness. They didn't care about race or age or religion. They didn't attack anyone. They did not tend to push people off of cliffs in the name of the Buddha.

I read recently that Buddhism is the fastest-growing religion in Australia. Bishop Piper of the Anglican Church promptly made a video warning against the evil "deception" of Buddhism.

When reporters asked for response from Reverend Shin, affiliated with the Nan Tien Temple, he said, "We don't convert people to Buddhism or change their religion. As long as they feel comfortable with any of the practices or any of the beliefs and it is good for the society, good for them and good for the family, that is the most important thing. Whether they decide to become Buddhists or not—that is not our concern."

Now, which one would you rather hang out with?

We were all grieving. We were all humans carrying around our mustard seeds.

This was my first inkling of what Barack Obama meant when he said "We are all one."

In *Zen and the Art of Happiness*, Chris Prentiss described the oneness of the world this way: imagine human beings are individuals frozen into different ice shapes, but in the end, we're all made out of water.

I wrote, "Some women on the Net said it didn't help to hear other people's terrible stories. They were depressed enough by their own. But I am always surprised and heartened to hear that I do not have a monopoly on misery. It's not just 'misery loves company,' although there's that too. But I feel most isolated when I think, *I am alone. I am the only one who has suffered.* When I see that other people have, too, I think, *Okay. This is not a malicious turn by the gods. This happens. You get through. They suffered, they got through. I'm suffering, I'll get through. One foot in front of the other.*

Slowly, carefully, I started to build a *sangha*, a community of other awakened beings who could help carry me through this.

Master Reverend Olo

My husband, Matt, was the pillar of my *sangha*, but after a week, he returned to work. My parents deluged me with food whenever they could. (Matt had to make four trips to the car when we left the hospital, because they had brought so much stuff: blankets, pillows, sushi, bananas, oranges, a bouquet of flowers ...) My friends, especially my cousin Karen, called whenever possible. But the other mainstay of my daily *sangha* was our puppy, Olo.

We'd adopted Olo from the SPCA the month before I got pregnant. Someone had boarded this little four-month-old golden retriever mix at the kennel and never came back for him.

I'd never had a dog before, and I was a bit worried at first. Would he like me? Didn't dogs just need lots of training and walking before they died? Even at four months, our first few "walks" were mostly him dragging me around by the leash, no matter how much I set in my heels and yelled at him to heel.

When we got back from the hospital and our puppy rolled on his back, seemingly unconcerned, I sobbed to Matt, "Why couldn't it have been him? Why couldn't Olo have died instead?"

Olo just looked at me with his dark eyes. In retrospect, I think it was a confusing time for him. He'd been shuttled to the hospital, had to wait in the car, had been shunted to my parents' house for a few days, then rejoined us at my brother's house. Once he got home, one of his humans often burst into tears, and the other seemed sad. Meanwhile, Olo was so little, he didn't even understand what tears were.

Yet Olo gave me exactly what I needed.

He didn't carry a grudge about my mean thoughts. He didn't even understand them. Now was now for him. When he was shut up in the back seat of our car, he was shut up. When he was outside, he was joyfully bounding through the snow. When he was asleep, he was asleep. That was what Buddhism was about, touching down and staying with the moment.

No fear. No anticipation. Just what is.

Olo listened. He loved to lie down while I stroked him and fondled his soft, yellow ears. He let me write every day, even every hour. He let me look after him. I wrote, "My dog just barfed a little. It wasn't too much barf. He let me pull the rope out that was gagging him. It gave me something to take care of. Just like if we'd had a healthy baby, I would have groaned at cleaning up the messes, but maybe secretly enjoyed it, because that's what I signed up for. To take care of my little boy or girl. Someone who would need me, whom I would nurture. Someone who would eventually grow up and leave both of us better people."

Olo also got me outside several times a day, skiing or walking in the woods.

Later, I read that going outside and surrounding yourself in nature elevates your mood. Even gazing at photos of trees made people feel better than looking at pictures of buildings and concrete. Thich Nhat Hanh already knew this, because in *Teachings on Love*, he suggested that psychotherapists talk to their clients while walking outside.

Now, I wasn't doing formal walking (or cross-country skiing) meditation. I wasn't conscious of how I tightened the laces of my ski boots or pushed off with my poles. But, for the love of Olo, I set off down our icy road. I blinked snowflakes out of my eyelashes. I let the cold air sear my lungs. And I cried.

Everything made me cry.

I cried when I hit our first downhill slope. I'd fallen down a flight of stairs two days before Isadora died, and at the time, my first thought had been for my baby.

Now my baby was dead. If I fell, it didn't matter.

Even so, I marched down the hill sideways in my skis instead of bombing down the slope.

We crossed the bridge. I skiied along the snowmobile path while Olo bounded ahead.

I used to think about Isadora in the woods all the time. I bubbled with secret joy. I was pregnant. I was going to have a baby. We hadn't told too many people, which somehow magnified my pleasure, like she was our delicious little secret.

Today, I cried out. "My baby! My baby!"

Olo looked at me. He knew the tone was wrong, but not much else.

We kept moving.

The last time I'd skiied while pregnant, I'd made it past a bend in the road, up a tiny hill, with Isadora inside me. I'd looked up into the clear, crisp, sunny February sky and spotted a woodpecker sitting in the bare branches of a tree.

We made it to the same small hill now.

No woodpecker today.

Okay. Maybe that woodpecker only came on special occasions, like the last time you go skiing with your baby daughter.

I tried to sing "You Are My Sunshine." For her.

My voice rasped. I broke off and cried.

Since we'd come home from the hospital, I'd avoided music. I couldn't sleep. But I could still walk or ski with Olo.

A few years before, a writer had told me that their Buddhist temple had a Master Reverend German shepherd. Buddhism was so inclusive that it did not discriminate wisdom or enlightenment based on species.

I loved that. And I loved my Master Reverend Olo.

Loving-kindness *(Metta)*

In *Lovingkindness: The Revolutionary Art of Happiness*, Sharon Salzberg says that it all starts with *metta*, which means love or loving-kindness. (She writes it as all one word, like it all flows together, which it kind of does. In an ideal world. But I prefer the hyphen, myself.)

Apparently *metta* is the first "heavenly abode," and so if you can get that down, you'll figure out the other abodes where compassion, sympathetic joy, and equanimity live.

She doesn't mean love in the usual Hollywood boy-meets-girl kind of way.

She meant loving unconditionally. Like if you poured water from a cup into a vase, the water would flow into a different shape, just like love could change form, but it was still all love.

Kate Braestrup did a great riff on this in her memoir, *Marriage and Other Acts of Charity*. She explained the Greek words for love. Just like the Inuit are supposed to have lots of words for snow, the Greek had a few different words for love. *Eros* was the Hollywood one, with all the up-all-night, can't-get-enough fireworks and banging. *Philos* was more steady and durable friendship. And *agape* was this unconditional love. The one that's patient and kind, the one that believeth in all things and endureth all things.

So *agape* is *metta* or loving-kindness. And you can kind of see how it would save the world.

Luckily, Buddhism even has a road map on how to increase your *metta*. (That sounds like a Buddhist Glamour Magazine title: Boost Your *Metta* Today!)

First, you start with meditating about someone you love. That fills you right up with loving-kindness, and your only job is to send even more loving-kindness toward your loved one.

Well, okay. I could do that.

I thought about my baby, my tiny little girl. Her skin had been translucent, so I could see the zigzag of red blood vessels underneath. Her eyelids were still fused closed, but I'd been amazed to see her miniature blond eyelashes. She also had a little bit of blond hair on her head as well as blond lanugo hair on her body ("She had fuzz," agreed Matt). I was so amazed to see any child of mine with blond hair. I'd counted her ten teeny fingers and ten wee toes.

My mother had held Isadora. The nurses had dressed her up in clothes for pictures, since volunteers will specially knit and sew outfits for babies who don't make it, but the hat and dresses were way too big for her small form.

I loved her.

The next step was to meditate on someone you felt neutral about, like a bank teller. I would try to summon up loving-kindness toward them.

My mind started to wander. I couldn't even decide whom to fixate on, since I didn't care about this person.

So I never made it to the last step, which was to think of someone you hated and send them loving-kindness too.

Mindfulness, Part II

I might be a little handicapped at Buddhism because medicine was not about mindfulness and loving-kindness.

Well, maybe there was some *metta* in medical school. But mostly med school was about stuffing facts into your brain, reciting them at appropriate intervals, and learning how not to stand when you could sit, sit when you could lie down, or lie down when you could sleep.

So you ended up with a really big brain, but divorced from your body and silly indulgences like hunger, thirst, or going to the bathroom.

But when I thought about it, I realized that med school did teach me one tiny piece of mindfulness.

I loved my general surgery rotation, mostly because the residents were having so much fun despite their insane schedules. As a med student, I was on call one in three, so every night, I was either on call (up all night), post-call (pushing myself for 36 hours or whatever because I'd been up all night), or pre-call (one glorious night where I'd eventually get to stumble into my own bed, but I'd be back at it in the morning).

That made me really appreciate the one night of pre-call.

One night that I'd get to see my husband before he was asleep.

One night that I'd get to take a shower in my own house.

Amazing.

If I worked nine to five and got to go home every night, I might start complaining about niggly little things, like a scuff on my shoe. But on general surgery, man. I'd only wear running shoes and cover them with surgical booties anyway, so I'd just feel intensely grateful if I ever got the chance to wear nice shoes at all.

Mindfulness.

In her memoir, *Marriage and Other Acts of Charity*, Kate Braestrup met a man whose wife had died of cancer. Right up to the bitter end, church members told him to pray and never give up hope, because God might turn up with a miracle any second. If the man tried to talk about her imminent death, they cut him off and acted like the illness was his fault for not having enough faith. After she died, the man stopped going to church ("No offense," he told Kate, who is a minister), and said that there are some things that prayer just can't fix. For example, if you're jumping out of an airplane at 30,000 feet without a parachute and planning to pray yourself to safety, chances are, it ain't going to happen.

He expected a lecture from Kate. Instead, she agreed with him that in that case, you were toast, and if it ever happened to her, it would be her final adventure. She hoped she could remember to be curious.

"Curious?" he said.

She wanted to pay attention to how it felt, since nothing else would happen to her in this lifetime again.

When I read that, I felt a smidgen little less afraid for the people who jumped out of the World Trade Center on 9/11. I still tear up when I think about them and their terrible choice between burning to death or jumping.

And I finally understood the koan (Zen riddle) about the tiger. I'm sure you've heard it. A man is fleeing a tiger who is intent on eating him. The man scrambles up a cliff to get away. He manages to cling to a vine, but a mouse starts to gnaw on the vine. The man's about to fall to his doom, consumed by the tiger, but first, he spots a strawberry dangling from the vine in front of him. He picks it and says, "How delicious!"

This story made absolutely no sense to me when I first heard it. "Sucks to be you," was about all I got out of it.

But when Kate said she would try to be curious if she fell out of an airplane, I finally got it. Sure, while tumbling out of an airplane, you might hope and strategize, but let's be honest, doom is doom. Death is death. You might as well face it head on.

Whenever I got on an airplane, I always considered the fact that I might not get out alive. Yes, sure, flying was safer than driving. But I was aware that things could go wrong and we might not all survive the flight. It made me very grateful when I rolled my suitcase onto the tarmac.

So I understood mindfulness better now. And I knew I should apply it to this very minute. That was the whole point.

But Isadora was dead.

Wouldn't it feel even more painful to stay conscious and aware of that, every moment?

But I Keep Having These Thoughts …

(Other Pregnant Women, Part II)

I made a new friend, which cheered me up so enormously that I called her my tiramisu. Not because she resembled the dessert, but the name is Italian for "to lift you up." We invited her and her boyfriend "Chipotle" over to our house for a barbecue.

They had barely cleared the threshold before Chipotle said, "Oh, you better tell them your announcement."

I held my breath. *Please do not tell me you're pregnant.*

"Oh, that's right." She turned to me, wide-eyed. "In the past week, I have become—"

Oh God, oh God.

"—a vegetarian."

I blinked at her. "Well, that's fine. We have veggie hot dogs and burgers."

"Great."

"But why didn't you tell me?"

"I forgot!"

I shook my head. "I thought you were going to tell me you were pregnant! Phew." Of course I couldn't stop my friends, enemies, or random celebrities from gestating, but I still dreaded it enormously.

What should I do with these negative thoughts?

One of my friends constantly worried that she didn't love her daughter enough. She said, "I wish I could just cut out that part of my brain, the part that has these thoughts!"

I looked at her. "But that wouldn't work."

"I know! But I wish it would!"

That didn't make any sense to me.

I had the same reaction when I read a book called *Crazy, Sexy Cancer Survivor*. I picked it up not because I had cancer, but because anyone who can combine the words "crazy sexy" and "cancer" was someone I'd like to talk to. (By the way, the best cancer memoir I ever read was *It's Not About the Hair: And Other Certainties of Life and Cancer*, by Debra Jarvis.)

Back to *Crazy, Sexy Cancer Survivor*. I liked most things about it, except where she talked about negative thoughts. She said to put an elastic band around your wrist and snap it every time you had a downer thought.

That made me uncomfortable.

I already knew that scolding myself didn't work. Pretending to be cheery and carefree didn't work either. And my pseudo-meditation hadn't cured me yet.

I got another clue from a different book, *The Dark Side of the Light Chasers*. I almost didn't pick it up because the title's cheesiness made me cringe, but the content made me think. The author, Debbie Ford, talked about this tendency to self-edit of parts of ourselves we don't like. She compared it to being born in a castle with thousands of rooms, but every time someone told you you'd done something wrong, you shut off the light to that room and locked the door.

For example, if your dad said, "Boys don't cry," you made darn sure you didn't cry anymore. Or "Girls shouldn't dress like sluts." Or whatever.

This book basically said that you had to accept all parts of yourself, and the parts that make you feel most ashamed are the ones you should pay most attention to. It was my first taste of Jungian philosophy.

I thought of my friends (women, of course) who denied their anger. "I'm not angry. I'm frustrated." "I'm irritated." "It's not that I'm angry, but ... "

Why didn't they just admit that they were pissed off so we could get it out in the open and be done with it?

Of course, I was the one who over-expressed anger.

Sylvia Boorstein said that someone asked His Holiness the Dalai Lama if he ever got angry.

He laughed (laughed!) and said, "Of course! Things happen that I don't want to happen and anger arises. But, it's not a problem."

"Anger arises."

He was not his anger.

He was not his thoughts.

Neither was I.

The thoughts came and went. No big deal.

I didn't have to start judging. "Uh oh, I shouldn't think that! It's bad juju to look at another woman's pregnant belly and sigh. Stop thinking it! Ahhh! You're thinking it again!"

Once I was able to detach myself and give myself permission to be jealous, envious, and covetous of other women's babies, I could forget about those feelings.

This key was one of Buddhism's secrets.

Give yourself permission, and it all goes away.

It worked for other people, too. In *The Chocolate Cake Sutra*, Geri Larkin said that when she eavesdropped on cell phone calls, three-quarters of the people were whining.

Geri whined a lot herself, and she wanted to stop. So she instructed herself to stop. It didn't work.

She told her young daughter to stop. It didn't work.

They decided to reward themselves with Barbie clothes and other treats if they managed to stop whining.

No deal. In fact, the repression just made them whine more.

But when they gave themselves permission to whine-o-rama, when they gave themselves an official whining hour per day—

Boom.

The end o' whining.

Thank you, Buddhism. I was about to put the theory to the test.

My maternity leave was up. I was returning to the emergency room.

Mustard Seeds at Work

I drove to the hospital in Montreal, crying almost the entire way. At the stoplights in Dorion and Ile-Perrot, I wiped my tears and studiously avoided any eye contact with other drivers. When I got closer, I started up a CD about cardiac resuscitation and steadied myself for a day at the emergency room.

The first person I saw was the chief of the emerg, whom I also considered my friend.

He said, "Good to have you back. We missed you. I told everyone you had a miscarriage and to leave you alone."

"Technically, it was a stillbirth, because she was over twenty weeks old."

"Right. Stillbirth."

It may have been a small difference to him, but I didn't know any women who took two months off for a miscarriage. Maybe some of them wanted to, especially if it was one of several losses. But a stillbirth meant you'd carried your baby past the danger point. You'd thought everything was going to be all right. You'd made all your plans and dreams. And then you delivered your dead baby.

I didn't believe in a hierarchy of loss, but I was a little uneasy that the other doctors had been misinformed right off the bat.

It was also bizarre that he'd told them to leave me alone, as if they were going to come at me with pitchforks. But I knew he was trying to protect me.

His eyes shifted from side to side. "Whatever you want, we'll give it to you."

Hmm. I imagined myself as a child emperor in oversized garments, waving my scepter. What I actually said was, "I'd like at least five shifts next month."

A cardiologist asked how I was doing. I said, "Well, okay." Awkward pause.

He said, "Well, at least it's great weather outside."

"Gorgeous," I agreed, relieved to move on.

As I grabbed a throat culture, another emergency doctor greeted me. "Good to see you again." He shook my hand. "*Really* good to see you again."

That touched me. We had never talked much before, but I could tell he meant it. It was exactly the right thing to say to me, not asking about what had happened, but welcoming me back.

Rain, the only nurse I had told I was pregnant, came by and gave me a hug. "Aw, I'm sorry, hon."

My face crumpled.

"Are you okay? Are you ready to come back to work, hon?"

I nodded. "It's just when people are nice to me."

"I understand. If you need anything, you let me know, okay?"

I nodded, looking at her through my tears. "I had a little girl."

"Aw, did you? That's great. You let me know if you need anything, okay?"

I said yes and tucked my head back down over my charting.

Another nurse said, "You were gone so long, I didn't think you were coming back!"

I forced a smile. I felt like staying away after a "miscarriage" made me sound like a wuss. But I realized it didn't really matter what they thought. I hadn't been working there too long and didn't know the group well. They had their own lives. Whether they cared or not, we would all move on.

Then I saw a mother with her first baby, a ten-month-old named Dora who had crawled off the change pad and hit her head, I caressed the baby's wispy blond hair, and a ribbon of sadness coursed through me.

A little girl baby with nearly the same name.

A playful, alert, and cheery baby. Her first-time mother was obviously distraught but pulling herself together.

I fought back the tears. I couldn't cry at work.

Working was hard. Sometimes it was hard in a good way. It did take my mind off Isadora, but it only delayed the mourning. It didn't replace it. I acted normal while eyeing my co-workers to check who would say something and who wouldn't. I was more tense. My sleep got screwed up. Work did leave me less time to obsess about procreation, but none of it was a panacea.

After a few shifts, I saw Michael Bellomo, a doctor who'd finished his residency a few years ahead of me. His brother had died in the Fall, so he had stopped shaving his beard, according to Jewish custom.

Michael had overheard about my pregnancy during happier times. "Are you WITH CHILD?" he'd half-yelled from the next cubicle.

This time, he said, "I'm so sorry," and he was.

My eyes filled with tears.

He said, "If there's anything I can do for you, a shift I can take for you .... You can come over to our house. We'll lend you our son, you can take him around ... anything. Just ask me."

Later, I called him. He told me about his own loss, how his brother died, how his parents were devastated, and his second cousin was born prematurely and nearly died in the same week.

Prior to this, Michael had attended the synagogue two or three times a year. But now he went twice a day. They said prayers for the deceased for the entire year following a death. There is a quorum for these prayers. There have to be at least ten men. So when he felt there was no point in getting out of bed, he still did it because they were counting on him.

I was curious. I wondered if I could visit the synagogue.

"Come! Everyone is welcome. It's an orthodox synagogue."

Now I felt a little uneasy. "With the men and women separate?"

"Yes."

Great. So I'd be sitting by myself. I tried again. "Is it in Hebrew?"

"Yes, but on Saturdays, the sermon is in English, and there's always food afterward. Food is very important in Jewish culture."

"It's important in Chinese culture, too!"

Much later, I heard Chief Rabbi Lord Jonathan Sacks summarize all Jewish Bible stories like this: "They tried to kill us. They failed. Let's eat."

My kind of people.

I told Michael now, "I'm glad. It's been three months"—13 weeks since Isadora died. I'd be 33 weeks now—"and I thought that was a long time, but now, it still hurts."

"Of course it does. And she was inside you. She was a part of you. You can't forget that. Three months is soon. My brother died in August, and it wasn't until November that I started feeling a little better."

I felt less alone. I was building my *sangha*.

What Is the Sound of One Hand Clapping?

I had heard of Zen koans, or paradoxical questions can't be solved logically, such as, "What was your face before your mother or father was born?" Or "What is the sound of one hand clapping?"

When my life was going swimmingly, koans didn't interest me too much. And I didn't go seek them out now, but one came to me when I tried to talk to my mother about Isadora after a big family lunch.

I said, "Thank you for telling my aunt about Isadora. I want to remember her as a happy pregnancy too."

My mother lit up. "Did I ever tell you about the Brazilian woman? She lives on our road." Thence followed a tale about this neighbour, how they exchanged plants and thank-you cards, etc.

My mother often launched into lengthy, seemingly unrelated stories. I waited for the punch line.

It turned out Mom had told this neighbour we lost the baby, and she replied, "My daughter lost her first one, and then she had four!"

Hope was good. But I wanted to talk about Isadora, not future fecundity. I tried again. "For Mother's Day, we're going to make a donation to the Ottawa Hospital."

"That's good. We're going to see you that day, anyway." She turned away, ready to wash more dishes.

I took a deep breath.

She whipped back toward me and hugged me. "It's okay."

I started crying.

She let go of me and disappeared without warning.

This, like her interminable stories, was expected. I searched for a paper towel, but then she returned with a box of tissues. I took one.

She started washing a pot, briskly. "Aunt Mary was worried about Grandma, too. That she's not eating."

I cried by myself behind her back. This wasn't working. I tried one more time. "Mom. Do you ever think about Isadora?"

She turned then. "A little. But you're young. You shouldn't dwell on it." She rinsed the pot one more time. "You shouldn't let it stop you."

I'm not stopped. I'm working. I'm writing. I do yoga. I haven't cracked up. But I still love my daughter, and I'm not ready to sweep her under the carpet.

Instead of saying that, though, all I could do was cry.

I was afraid that in the end, Matt and I would be alone in our grief. And then, at the eleventh hour, I would be the only one.

My mother would rather wash dishes than talk about Isadora.

She placed the pot on the drying rack. "If you want, we can have a ceremony once a year."

There it was. Carefully contained mourning. An annual pass.

I wandered out to the living room. Matt read my face and mouthed, "Are you okay?"

I shrugged and headed downstairs. I held it together until we were alone in the car, driving toward Shoppers City West. Then I let the tears pour out. Once he parked the car, I could not stop. Huge, seizing, breakthroat tears.

In the end, we were alone. My friends weren't calling or writing as much. We got a good outpouring of support, but now it was trickling away. My own parents thought we should march on into the future, pump out babies, and forget about her except for one day a year.

"It's just us," I sobbed. "It's not right."

Someone had to remember her. Just us wasn't enough. Even if one writer friend had circled Isadora's birthday on her calendar. Even if others had prayed. I wanted permanent, continual, whole-hearted remembrance of my little girl.

I sat there, crying and crying, steaming up the windows, while shoppers zoomed their cars into parking spaces or reversed out of the lot around us.

Matt tried to console me. Olo watched me for a while, then settled in his seat with a sigh.

Matt agreed. It was just us. But he didn't seem to find it excruciating. He never expected it to be otherwise.

I raged. "What is the sound of one hand clapping? I've heard a few explanations, and they all make sense, but I think it's our daughter! We're parents, but we're not parents. We have a daughter, but we don't have a daughter. She lived, but she died. We remember her, but we can't have her. The intention was there, but we never got to keep her. She is the one hand clapping!"

Matt stared at me. "I don't understand."

"Well, what do you think it means, one hand clapping?"

"I think it was something made up by monks living in a cave, who don't get enough to eat!"

It didn't make concrete sense. I knew that. But I understood that koan now, in a terrible way. I felt like Isadora was also the answer to another popular question: if the tree falls in the forest without anyone to hear it, did the tree fall?

Did our daughter exist? Does she count? Does she matter? Or is she the one hand, forever clapping, but we can't hear her from our dimension?

I asked, "Do you feel it as hard as I do?"

He shook his head. "No. I don't think so."

So, in the end, I was alone. He just supported me as best he could. And I supported myself. And most of the time, I was okay.

I was just one hand, clapping.

Other Pregnant ... Men?

Or, Choose Your Ingredients

I started out one shift with a fellow doctor, whom I'll call Bob, smiling extra hard at me. "I'm sorry. How are you doing?"

I could hardly answer. It was too painful. I thanked him.

Fifteen minutes later, he told me he wouldn't be concentrating much today because he had good news.

"What's that?"

He pulled a white plastic rectangle out of his pocket. I stared at it.

It was a pregnancy test with two lines. A positive pregnancy test.

"Congratulations," I said, on cue. I knew he already had several children.

"If all goes well," he said.

I knew he was trying to downplay it for me, but it left a false residue in my mouth. Most pregnancies are fine.

All day long, I overheard him present his test and show it off to other doctors, nurses, and secretaries.

"How are you, Doctor?"

"Well, you know, I had to have a few tests today."

"Oh, no. Why is that?"

"I had to have ... this!" And he'd whip out the test and explain how he'd brought his wife's urine to the lab that morning, and Bob's your uncle! (Or, in this case, a very happy father-to-be.)

Next, he started asking if we'd mind if he finished his shift early so he could celebrate. Of course we all said, go, go.

I wrote afterward, "It's bad enough to see other women who are pregnant. I didn't anticipate listening to proud papas as well. Which I know is crazy because I wish all dads were as loving and involved, but do I have to work with them?"

Also, I wondered why they wouldn't take a home pregnancy test instead of transporting her urine to the hospital.

So. Did Buddhism have any wisdom to offer on this score? Actually, yes.

My first instinct was to avoid this doctor and drip candle wax into my ears so I wouldn't have to hear him for eight hours at a time.

But in *Instructions to the Cook*, authors Bernard Glassman and Rick Fields suggested that life is like making a recipe. Say you don't like cloves because their smell overpowers you. Fair enough. You don't have to use them. Just like you don't have to hang out with a sappy, smarmy businessman who pads his expense accounts.

But cloves might come in handy sometime. Maybe you don't want a giant clove sticking out of your hamburger bun, but a tiny shaving might elevate your pumpkin pie. And that bum-kissing businessman might have a lot of contacts to raise money for charity.

If the ingredient truly doesn't fit, leave it out. Recognize that it might have its place and you'll probably have to use it sometime, just not right now.

This was a revelation for me. What? Instead of raging against the machine, stewing, and pointing out various flaws to other people, I should just ... walk away?

Huh.

I did walk away already. I rarely make a scene, especially at work or in front of people I hardly know. The problem was that I walked away silently gnashing my teeth. Really, I was biding my time until I could complain to someone I did know, usually my husband, who would just listen.

Or laugh.

Actually, that was what happened in this case. I told my friend Isabel, "He was flashing his wife's urine pregnancy test. He was carrying it around in his pocket all day. Doesn't that seem kind of ... unsanitary?"

"Yes!" she said.

We giggled.

And that was how I finally let go of the pregnant man. Permission to steam and then laugh.

Isabel

I have to say a few more things about my friend Isabel. We had gone to med school together. She was intelligent, well-spoken, and extremely kind, but I knew she was a devout Christian, which always made me hang back a little for fear of sermons and self-righteousness.

However, when I slowly, subconsciously assembled my mustard seed *sangha*, Isabel was key.

For example, I'd asked Karen, my cousin, one of my million-dollar questions. "How can I be happy without forgetting Isadora?"

Karen said, "Mmm, nope. You're going to have to work through that one yourself." It was the same thing the priest had said, that I'd have to learn how to forgive myself.

I wrote, "I guess it's true, but I wish someone had the magic wand to lay on me."

Isabel wasn't a magic wand, but the mustard seed *sangha* was the closest I could get. I drew enormous comfort from the women online who'd gone through the same thing. I often called the doctor who'd had a full-term stillborn baby girl. And I loved the wise mother-friends who weren't afraid of my grief and walked alongside me.

One of the latter was my friend Isabel.

She was like a wise Magic 8-Ball. She could deliver intelligent, profound answers with complete faith and reason and compassion.

Me: Am I a mother?

Isabel: You are a mother. You carried her, you delivered her, you love her. There is nothing else to it. (In fact, nearly everyone, especially my friends with kids, called me a mother. It was mostly my own mind that had excluded me.)

Me: Where is she?
Isabel: All babies go straight to heaven.
(I still didn't believe that, but I was comforted by Isabel's certainty.)

Me: What is heaven?
Isabel: I envision heaven as a place of complete joy and complete understanding beyond our comprehension .... I think she's with Juan, my brother, right now!

I was so touched. I had vaguely imagined that if heaven existed, Isadora would be with her grandparents. People often say stuff like, "She's with dear Uncle Louie now," so I'd subconsciously pictured little families hanging out in the Great Beyond. But here was my friend saying that her brother would look out for Isadora, too. Suddenly, heaven seemed like a friendlier place.

I wrote, "Faith is a wonderful thing. Faith combined with reason and compassion really makes you feel better. You don't have to mourn as much if you think life goes on and is, in fact, even better afterward."

The only problem was, I couldn't make that leap of faith. Hence my struggle.

Me: Maybe Isadora was really scared. I never got to tell her that I love her.
Isabel: I think babies know they are loved and wanted. Through your voice, through your heartbeat, through your hormones a little too. You will meet her again. We'll all meet her. We just have to wait a little longer.

Me: I feel so helpless. I can't help her.

Isabel: All we can do is first, love our children, and second, do our best for them.

I'd expected her to say something like, *Well, no wonder. You are helpless.* This was much better. I did love Isadora and I had tried to do my best for her.

Thank you, Isabel.

The $86,400 Question

Patients were angry, as usual. One man came back to see a specialist who didn't want to see him, so the patient bounced back to the emergency doctor. I picked up the chart and, about two seconds into the history, I realized a) the patient didn't speak English almost at all, and b) his adult daughter was furious because she'd waited all day to see an emergency doctor plus a specialist the day before. Today the daughter had waited again, both times with her toddler in tow.

The obvious solution for the daughter was to take it out on me, especially when the patient said he was having more pain in his stomach and felt faint, so I ordered an electrocardiogram and blood test to make sure he wasn't having a heart attack.

"Do you know what it's like to wait eight hours with a child?" the daughter said,

I said I was sorry, but the best thing for her father was to investigate. "I know it sounds strange, but any pain in that area can be suspicious. If the results are normal, you can all go home."

"Do you know what it's like to wait in the waiting room with a child?" the daughter repeated.

"Ma'am, if you don't want to stay, you don't have to, but it's really your father's decision. You'll have explain it to him and then sign a letter that you're leaving against medical advice. This is what I do with all patients who have any sort of chest pain, who almost faint."

"Do you have children?"

The million-dollar question. I thought I did. Many people didn't. The two-million-dollar question was, did it matter what other people thought?

I said, "I don't think that's relevant. Why don't I leave you and your father to discuss this?" I closed the door behind me.

She followed me out in the hall and pursued me to the doctors' desks. "Do you have children? Do you? Do you?"

I still didn't know what to say when patients asked if I had children. Isabel had suggested, "I had a daughter, and she died," but it was none of this woman's business.

In the end, the daughter agreed to an electrocardiogram without a blood test. But what I really remembered was that I stayed calm.

I didn't shout, "No, I don't know what it's like to wait with a child. I wish I did!"

I didn't burst into tears.

The whole incident didn't bother me as much as it could have. If anything, I thought the daughter was out of line for asking me questions that she would never dare (okay, she would hesitate to) ask an older, male doctor. In retrospect, I might have defused the situation by lavishly sympathizing with her and lathering her in apologies for her long stay in the ER the previous day. But in another, more honest way, I didn't feel like it.

I had enough problems. Still, I was able to close off my emotions when people attacked me.

One hug, and I was still ready to blub, yet I could stay calm in the face of adversity.

In *Lessons of the* Lotus, Bhante Y. Wimala pointed out that every day contains eighty-six thousand and four hundred seconds. He said to think of them like dollar bills. Each day, you have $86,400 to spend. How would you like to spend them?

I was spending my dollars a little more calmly.

As Isabel had said, "Our days are finite." I was not going to spend my days or seconds scrapping with patients' families, if I could help it.

Equanimity, Part II

Here is a pond so clear and fresh that you look at the bottom and you could trace the wrinkles in each rock with your big toe. A leaf floats on the surface. All is calm.

A crab scuttles into the pool, escaping a predator. Silt rises, so black that you can no longer see your feet or anything else.

The crab hunkers down, safe.
The silt settles.
The pond water clears.
You can see again.

That's equanimity, as envisioned by Bhante Y. Wimala. Equanimity doesn't mean bad stuff never happens to you. It doesn't mean that you don't feel anger, sadness, or sing-out-loud, bust-a-rhyme, one hundred percent love and joy. You feel all these things. But in between, you return to calm more easily.

Have you ever poured a tablespoon of salt into a glass of water and tried to drink it? Sucks, right? It doesn't matter if you add pretty blue food colouring or even a shot of tequila. It's still yuck. But if you poured that tablespoon of salt into the ocean, NBD. The ocean would taste the same.

In other words, you can't change the fact that somewhere, sometime, someone will dump salt in your water, but you can alter your reaction to the salt, whether you're more like the glass of water or the ocean. That was how Sharon Salzberg and Thich Nhat Hanh both described equanimity.

Sharon also wrote that after a week of meditation on loving-kindness, or *metta*, she didn't notice any difference except feeling guilty that she'd spent the entire week aiming *metta* toward herself. But then she dropped a jar. Usually, she would castigate herself, but now her first thought was, *You really are a klutz, but I love you.*

Hmm. I definitely wasn't there yet.

May You Be Happy

I knew I was a worry-a-holic, or as Sylvia Boorstein put it, full of restlessness and fretting. I also knew it was part of my programming. Perhaps genetic, certainly familial, since both my mother and grandmother habitually woke up at 3 a.m. to worry.

I read a cute little book called *Better Than Chocolate: 50 Proven Ways to Feel Happier*, by Siimon Reynolds.

Naturally, one way to feel happier was meditation. He had a simple way to do it, too. Pick a word like "peace" or "calm" or "love" and say it to yourself for ten or twenty minutes.

Even I could do that. I picked peace. That was what I most needed. I lay on my back and put crystals on my belly, because one of my Internet friends had suggested it, and I needed all the help I could get.

Peace, peace, peace.

I wondered if I should pray, too.

Anne Lamott pointed out that her most useful prayers were "help me, help me, help me" and "thank you, thank you, thank you." That made sense to me. (Anne Lamott was one of only two Christian writers I could read without gagging. Her book, *Traveling Mercies: Some Thoughts on Faith*, also contained the world's best essay on grief, "Ladders.")

I decided to pray at Isadora's place, Buddhist style.

After the ground thawed and Matt finished the purpleheart box, we buried Isadora's ashes on her due date, July 15th. Matt built a cairn of rocks over the spot. We planted greenery around her, including oak tree saplings, Minnesota snowflake bushes, and a blue spruce tree for Christmas. Wild strawberries and blackberries flourished around her.

Olo rushed ahead of me, crashing onto the neighbour's property. He'd abandoned his bone halfway to her site. Was that sacrilege? Should I pick it up?

After a minute, I decided that Olo, too, was leaving a tribute, and carried on.

I walked clockwise around Isadora's grave eight times and chanted, "May you be happy, may you be free from suffering."

I walked clockwise another eight times and chanted, "May we be happy, may we be free from suffering." (It was supposed to be "May I be happy, may I be free from suffering," but my throat just closed up if I even thought about saying that. It was too much like the woman who sent herself flowers on her twins' birthday/death day instead of sending flowers to their grave site.)

I walked clockwise two last times and chanted, "May all beings be happy. May all beings be free from suffering." That felt right. No one should suffer. I thought often of other women who had lost babies and had struggled to conceive. Sometimes, I named them while I walked.

It helped.

But What About Isadora?

The minister, Eleanor, who asked I was being gentle with myself, also asked if I talked to Isadora.

"Sort of," I said. Mostly, I'd cried, "I love you, I miss you, I'm sorry!"

I'd imagined her tiny voice peeping back, "Mommy, don't let me go!"

This was not a comfort.

I asked my wise, kind Wiccan friend, Leslie, for help. She said she prayed for Isadora and me and Matt. She suggested visualizations.

1. Pour yourself a glass of water. Imagine it filled with love and compassion. When it's full, drink it up.

2. Take a shower. Imagine the water washing the grief and depression away. When you turn off the water, imagine the sun burning away the last traces of sadness. Say your name three times.

3. When you go to bed, imagine the moon shining on you and the Goddess/Creator taking you in her arms. Leslie said it helped her sleep.

I read this e-mail several times. I was glad she had sent it. But my first thought was, *This is all about me. What about Isadora?*

People mostly seemed to worry about me and Matt, but not about our daughter.

I knew Isadora was gone. But in my mind, she was paramount. Everyone should pay rapt attention to my baby. We would never forget her. We would never leave her.

So if my friends called and we didn't talk about her, for me, it was like I had a sucking chest wound, but they were commenting on my jeans or asking if I'd seen the cute "popcorn kittens" video. That stuff was okay, but it wasn't Isadora.

I walked to the bookcase and gathered two blankets. The first was a handkerchief my father had embroidered with her full name, Isadora Jane Yuan Innes. The second was a silk shawl my friend Beatrice had given me "in honour of your motherhood, present and future."

I pressed the blankets against my chest. With my free hand, I rang a brass handbell that we'd rung on our wedding day. I cried and said her name.

The bell's peals died down. I felt more peaceful. Now I could pay attention to myself.

I already had a glass full of water. I carried it to our back window where I could almost, but not quite, spy the two ash trees surrounding Isadora's place.

I tried to picture love and compassion in my glass, but the liquid was clear. It didn't look like anything.

Okay. I could work with it. I imagined that the clear liquid represented the purity of love and the simple depth of compassion.

I drank it all.

The sun was setting. Gray dusk breathed across the sky. I felt melancholy but more tranquil.

Music

At first, I didn't listen to music. I cried so much, music wouldn't have made much difference anyway.

The only problem was, the few songs I'd heard earlier got stuck in my brain. Like "1985," by Bowling for Soup, replayed endlessly, making for horrible "ear worms."

I'd heard "1985" numerous times while driving to and from my emergency room shifts with Isadora in my belly. I'd sing along at top volume, wondering if she could hear me or feel the vibrations.

The song reminded me of her. Everything reminded me of her.

So, just like giving myself permission to whine, I gave in to listening to music.

I made an iPhoto slideshow of Isadora's photos and played "Here Without You," by 3 Doors Down in the background. And I made up a playlist for Isadora. It helped.

Songs That No One Else Would Cry To

"1985," by Bowling for Soup

"Slow Motion," by Juvenile

"Hey Mama," by the Black Eyed Peas (I'd named my "Congratulations, you're pregnant" e-mail folder "Hey Mama.")

Songs That Expressed the Darkness

"Here Without You," by 3 Doors Down
"Broken," by Seether, featuring Amy Lee
"Welcome to My Life," by Simple Plan
"Boulevard of Broken Dreams," by Green Day

Songs About Tenderness and the Crazy, Back-and-Forth Dance of Grieving and Rebuilding

"Breathe," by Anna Nalik (heard this on the radio when we were driving to the funeral home to make arrangements)
"You Were Meant for Me," by Jewel
"Song Instead of a Kiss," by Alannah Myles
"Over and Over," by Nelly, featuring Tim McGraw (because it's about lost love, plus I recognized the vicious circle of my thoughts endlessly replaying in my head)
"Hazy Shade of Winter," by the Bangles
"I Wish It Would Rain Down," by Phil Collins
"Separate Lives," by Phil Collins and Marilyn Martin
"Day by Day," by Doug and the Slugs
The Mission soundtrack, by Ennio Morricone

I listened to Sarah McLachlan's *Fumbling Toward Ecstasy* and *Surfacing*. The lyrics tore at me. But I was able to listen and even chime in.

Slowly, over time, I allowed myself to take comfort in music.

The music became part of my *sangha*, too.

Permission to Mourn Melissa-style

One of the weird things about grief, especially when I didn't belong to any religious tradition, was that no one would tell me if I was doing anything wrong, or anything right. I knew what I didn't believe in, but not what I did. Mostly, I worried that no one could guarantee me that Isadora was okay.

I was still in freefall.

When I thought about Michael Bellomo praying twice a day at his synagogue, I felt guilty. Should I pray twice a day, too? Did I need a certain number of people to pray in order to make it official? What should I do?

I still felt guilty when I felt flashes of happiness.

My baby was dead. How could I be happy?

In *Don't Bite the Hook*, Pema Chödrön encouraged cheerfulness. She said it was a habit you should strengthen by choosing to notice small, happy details. For me, that might be the softness of Olo's ears or the sunlight on my face.

She said anger was a habit, too.

Fortunately, I spoke to my friend Elyanne about all this. Elyanne was an assistant professor and a specialist in pediatric research, but I remembered when we were in undergrad together and she was enamoured of Immanuel Kant and the proletariat struggle.

I mentioned my nebulous sadness and grief whenever someone else announced a pregnancy.

Elyanne found it perfectly normal. "I have a friend who had two miscarriages. Not quite the same thing, but she said every time she sees a pregnant woman or hears about a positive pregnancy test, she goes through the loss all over again." That person put up with a lot of insensitivity, including a "friend" who responded to her e-mail about miscarriage with "That's too bad. Hey, I have news. I'm pregnant!"

Elyanne told me, "Maybe you have to work out your grief now. Then, when it's time, you will get pregnant. I'm hoping my best for you."

Elyanne believed in some sort of life after death. I was astonished to hear that a few times, when she was extremely close to a patient, she would finish up at the hospital and head home to rest, only to wake up in the middle of the night and say, "Oh. That child is gone," and go back to sleep. When she returned to the hospital in the morning, the patient would have passed away overnight.

"Really?"

"Sure. If I was really close to the patient and the family."

"Really?"

"Yes. A couple of times."

She found it unremarkable, but I was awed. I wished I could say definitively, "This moment is when Isadora's spirit left her body." You'd think if anyone could, I would. After all, she was inside me. But I wasn't attuned to the spirit world. Like, at all.

I told Elyanne the stress of having to live up to BID (twice a day) praying, Jewish style. Elyanne didn't see any obligations or strictures for how I was supposed to mourn. "I think you'll find your own way of doing things. Whatever feels right for you. It sounds like being outdoors is really important to you. I can hear nature sounds and water around you. So maybe you can go for a walk and think of Isadora. But I don't think you have to do anything. You'll figure it out."

After talking to Elyanne, I relaxed. She had given me permission to mourn my way.

Funny, eh? I shouldn't need that kind of permission. But just like author Natalie Goldberg said that writers seem to subconsciously need permission from another writer to really feel free to write, I needed permission to mourn in my own crazy, patchwork, Buddhish way. And Elyanne gave it to me.

Koan: Loving and Losing

> I hold it true, whate'er befall
> I feel it when I sorrow most;
> 'Tis better to have loved and lost
> Than never to have loved at all.
> —Alfred Lord Tennyson

Was it really better to have loved and lost our baby?

Tennyson thought so.

I asked Matt.

He said, "I don't know."

I turned the question over and over in my mind.

I reread Sylvia Boorstein's *It's Easier Than You Think*. She said that life was challenging. She didn't like to say "suffering," but she recognized that love meant you would be hurt. It was inevitable. But you loved anyway.

So while my heart cried out, I'm hurt!, the Buddhist reply seemed to be, *Yes, we all hurt.*

I lost my baby!

Yes. You lost your baby.

I love her!

Yes. You love her.

She's gone!

Yes. She's gone.

I found that comforting because at least Buddhism acknowledged my pain. It didn't try and sweep my grief away or shape it into something it wasn't, like "It's all for the best" (for whom?) or "She's with God now" (can you guarantee me that?).

I wrote, "Buddhism just says, *Yes. Stay with it.* Until, eventually, I can pull myself out. It will take many, many tries, but I should be able to deal with it."

Still, I didn't feel enlightened or anything. I wrote, "I see that I'm a better person since having Isadora. Yeah, I'm more sensitive to death. Yeah, I gave the first guy a note for work without demanding ten dollars. Yeah, I felt more sensitive to the depressed woman who came to emerg. Whoopie. It doesn't convince me losing Isadora was a worthwhile or good thing."

So, fully aware of my unenlightened, messy, entrails-exposed state, I asked myself again, *Would you rather Isadora hadn't existed at all, in order to spare yourself this pain?*

No.

No, of course not.

I would rather suffer a thousand times, a million times, for her.

I wrote, "Is it better to have loved and lost Isadora? I say so. She's still our miracle baby."

I turned my gaze to my big, sleepy yellow dog, asleep at my feet. I wrote "If we didn't love Olo, we wouldn't have to worry about losing him, either. But I do love him, even though chances are, he's going to die before me. After a certain point—no, after any point—not daring to love is diminishing. It's just fear."

Show Me the Pain

Almost three months after Isadora died, I had a dream where I tried to remember exactly how she looked.

I could summon up her face and her dear little head, her tiny torso and her flexed arms and legs, but try as I might, I could not absolutely recall the shape of her buttocks.

This really upset me. Now we would never know what her bum looked like. Like the rest of her, it was gone forever.

When I woke up, I sought out Matt in the shower. "Do you remember what Isadora's bum looked like?"

He burst out laughing under the spray. "No!"

"Do you remember turning her over and looking at it?"

He shook his head, still laughing.

"But now her bum is gone!" We'd never taken a picture of it, so it was really, really gone.

"Oh, the lost buttocks," he crooned, rinsing the shampoo out of his hair.

I was pretty sure I'd turned her over and checked her bum. It's part of the normal newborn exam, checking for a perforate anus. I even had vague memories of doing it two ways. I'd rolled her on her side and admired her tiny shoulder blades and her spine as well as her miniature buttocks. I also thought I'd lifted her legs in the air and peered at her from the underside.

I'm sure non-medical person would've thought I was a psychopath, but I wanted to check her all over so that I would remember every square millimetre of her.

And now, in my dream and in real life, I'd already started to forget her shape.

I couldn't hold on to her forever. She was leaving me.

In *Everyday Zen*, Charlotte Joko Beck described a conversation with a woman who was furious at what her husband had done three weeks ago.

Joko said, "Where is he?"

"He's at work. But he said—"

"What is it? Show it to me."

"I'm not showing you, I'm telling you. He said—"

"Show me."

"I can't. It's not here," the woman said, finally.

"Well, then," said Joko.

Her point was that whatever you're remembering is not happening right now. Look at what's happening right now.

What was happening right now, apart from me forgetting the contours of my daughter's buttocks?

Shortly after the lost bum dream, I woke up at 6 a.m. I saw Matt's sleeping face turned toward mine. It took my breath away for a moment.

He looked like Isadora.

It was the shape of his philtrum, that small indentation below the nose and above the lips, where angels are said to have pressed a kiss.

It was the slight overhang of his upper lip over his lower lip.

It was his closed eyes.

How strange, how happy-sad, how bitter and sweet and mournful and lovely, to be able to see my daughter in my husband's sleeping face.

It meant she was never completely gone from me.

Joko would probably not approve. I was still clinging, still craving, still wailing and suffering. But I was also learning how to let go, or at least stop clenching so hard that my palms bled.

On the other hand, every time I thought, *Okay, now I'm so much better. It's been a week/a month/fill in the blank. I must be better.* But something would throw me off.

At the end of yoga, during relaxation, I thought of Isadora, including my mother saying, "You'll be a good mother. Just not to this one."

I wrote, "But I'm still her mother, and I'm trying as hard as I can to be a good mother!"

If someone had seen my face during that "relaxation," they would have seen it crumple up as tears pricked my eyelids.

Busy-ness kept my grief at bay, but whenever I stopped, whenever I had time to myself, the rebound hit.

But with less power than before.

I wrote, "It's like a wave striking the shore. First, it hit me so hard, it rendered me breathless. Now, I still feel the wave strike me and I turn with it, but it doesn't shock and horrify and threaten me the way it once did. I remember the day after we lost her, when I thought of her punching and wiggling on ultrasound the week before .... I hyperventilated. I shook the bed with my sobs.

"Now, I can think of her on ultrasound and it might dim my mood or it might make me laugh, depending on how I feel. She was here. She was real. She was so beloved and right."

If Joko asked me to show her the pain, I might point to my heart.

But the pain was starting to ease a little.

That made me feel both better and worse.

More Wisdom From Isabel

Me: If I stop crying as much, what would Isadora think?
Isabel: She would be happy. She loves you and she wants you to be happy, too.

Me: I'm scared we'll never have another baby.
Isabel: All the professional women I saw at Women's College didn't start a family until they were in their late thirties. You started early. My mother had me when she was 40 and my brother when she was 43. And we're fine.

Me: But we've been trying for so long, one of my friends mentioned in vitro fertilization (IVF).
Isabel: You'd consider in vitro?! [Pause] I think these are ways of trying to get control when there is no control. We don't have control over when babies come.

Me: I'm upset every time a woman announces her pregnancy on the boards (online community).
Isabel: I think that's normal. And it's not really that you're mad at them; it's that you're unhappy for yourself. If you were pregnant, you'd be delighted for them.

Me (obviously feeling better and changing the subject a little): I'm reading about meditation, but I don't really get how it's supposed to help the world.
Isabel: It's not that I think you should sit and think and ignore the rest of the world. To the contrary, I think if you see

injustice, you should try and correct it. But if you spend your time praying and reflecting, you naturally want to do the right thing. You will be inclined toward doing what needs to be done and making the world a better place.

Part III

Creating a New Story

I do not look for love that is a dream—
 I only seek for courage to be still ...

—"Lady Montrevor," by Christina Rossetti

Haiku as Mindfulness

I started writing haiku after rereading *Seeds From a Birch Tree*, by Clark Strand.

I'd written a few haiku starting in grade three. What teacher doesn't love ye olde structure of a line made up out of five syllables, followed by one that's seven syllables, and then back to one of five syllables?

Clark Strand's haiku followed the same path, except he said you should mention the season and concentrate on the present moment in each poem.

I loved a lot of the poems, especially the one written in jail. When Clark gave a workshop in prison, the inmates said, "It's pretty hard to get in touch with the seasons when you're locked up." They meditated in an empty concrete room that was so hot, a fly wavered when it buzzed around the room. But one of them, Jakko Medina, wrote a wonderful haiku about the coolness of the water from the tap.

If he could write poetry under those circumstances, I could write under mine.

I took Olo for a walk. I kept my eyes open. I surveyed the trees. I noted my feet crunching on the snow and gravel and the wind cutting my cheeks. And I composed haiku in my head, shaving syllables here, expanding them there, to fit the form.

In June, I wrote a poem, not a haiku, that felt like a prayer.

Fireflies.
Tiny, tangible,
Transient stars,

Shine on my daughter.

I wanted to express the wonder of walking Olo at night, hand-in-hand with Matt, and seeing those little, moving sparks of white light.

Years later, I picked up Clark Strand's book again and realized that I wasn't doing haiku any more. Facebook statuses and tweets had supplanted them.

I figured that was all right. Status updates had the same spirit, anyway. After all, they were an answer to the same question, namely, "What are you doing right now?" I could post my answer. Sometimes I posted a haiku as my status/tweet.

Only it wasn't the same. As in the rest of my life, I tried to cram too much information into each sound bite. And I found that subconsciously, the whole "like" and "comment" and "retweet" thing, jockeying for attention and popularity, interfered with my ability to just post.

I needed to get back to basics.

Is This the Truth?

I still had so many thoughts. Dreadful, painful, self-excoriating thoughts.

Sharon Salzberg wrote about this in *Lovingkindness: The Revolutionary Art of Happiness*. She told her teacher that whenever she meditated, she kept remembering terrible things she had done.

Her teacher, Sayadaw U Pandita, responded, Well, are you finally seeing the truth about yourself?

Sharon was taken aback. Was she really this horrible person who had caused so much pain? Was that the entire picture of herself? After a minute, she said, No, that wasn't the truth.

Her teacher said, Stop thinking about it, then.

His advice was that simple.

That impossible.

Or was it? My husband seemed to manage.

I took a deep breath. I wanted to forgive myself. This was part of the deal.

I remembered my first encounter with Zen thought in the book, *Writing Down the Bones*, by Natalie Goldberg.

I loved her stories. I loved her writing advice. But something else stuck with me: she was afraid of loneliness.

Of course! I thought when I read that. *What if you didn't get married and you grew old alone and ended up addled, wearing a diaper, in a wheelchair, in a nursing home? Who* wouldn't *be afraid of loneliness?*

Katagiri Roshi, her teacher, said, "Well, what do you do when you're alone?"

Natalie observed herself and noticed that she did normal stuff, washing dishes and whatnot. It wasn't too scary.

She said, "But Roshi, aren't you afraid of loneliness? Don't you have those thoughts?"

"Of course," he said. "But they are just thoughts. I don't let them toss me away."

Huh.

Author Martha Beck calls the mind a two-bit whore because it tends to get caught up in biases and ego. She suggests listening your body, which tenses up around bad stuff and relaxes around the good stuff.

I thought yoga was helping me tune into my body, but the meditation and letting go of my thoughts were obviously still a problem.

When the Fifth Patriarch of Zen in China wanted to find his successor, he asked them all to write a verse explaining our original, Buddha nature.

The head monk wrote that the body was the tree of wisdom and the mind was a mirror that we had to polish at all times.

Everyone thought that was pretty good, until one illiterate man dictated a verse that in the end, there was no tree of wisdom and no mind, just emptiness. He was made the Sixth Patriarch of Zen.

I didn't really understand that emptiness.

Clearly, I was still back at the brain-polishing stage. I knew everyone was probably sick of hearing me talk about the possibilities of my past or future babies, but it was my own, life-altering koan and I had to keep shovelling away at it.

In twelfth-century China, an artist drew ten paintings of ox herding that have become a metaphor for enlightenment ever since. Training one's mind is like trying to tame an ox.

The first painting showed a figure casting about, confused and disillusioned. She was searching for the ox and couldn't find it anywhere. That was the beginning of the spiritual journey.

Been there. Done that. I called it freefall. Same thing.

In the second painting, the figure had located the ox's tracks, so at least she knew that the ox existed.

Hm. That would be me picking up the books on Buddhism.

In the third painting, the figure glimpsed the ox with her own eyes. Aha! The ox immediately ran away, but at least the person could see for herself that the ox was for real. At this stage of training the mind, the person became painfully aware of past errors and misguided judgments.

Ooh. Gotcha.

In the fourth painting, the figure caught up to the ox, but could not tame it. The mind remained too tense or slipped away when the person tried to gain control of it.

Hmm.

In the fifth painting, the figure had tamed the ox. The ox was still willful, but manageable. The person had become more at ease with her original, Buddha nature and could continue to progress beyond the average mind.

If I was lucky, I was probably in the third or fourth painting, just glimpsing the ox or maybe desperately trying to tame it.

Not bad.

Gentleness

"You can search throughout the entire universe for someone who is more deserving of your love and affection than you are yourself, and that person is not to be found anywhere. You yourself, as much as anybody in the entire universe, deserve your love and affection."—Buddha

I borrowed a book called *Sex, Soul & Synchronicity*, by Gail Vibe.

She said to pamper yourself once a day, every single day. A good way to do this was to ask, "What would I like? What do I need?" and then do it.

Forget work. Forget the dirty dishes.

Fifteen minutes to lie down on the lawn and watch the clouds drift through the sky.

Fresh flowers.

A ripe mango.

Chocolate.

She bought herself birthday and Christmas presents every year.

And if you were going through a crisis, she said it was even more important to be kind to yourself.

"Give yourself permission," she wrote.

I reread this page a dozen times. It felt so foreign, it was almost like decoding a different language.

I thought back to first year med school, when you really could study 24 hours a day and still not know everything. One friend said, "I study three hours a night and then I stop." Another friend said, "I make sure I do something fun every night, even if it's only making strawberry muffins."

At the time, I thought they were onto something, but I wasn't smart enough to follow their lead. I kept up my usual manic, burnout study pattern.

Well, better late than never. I decided to tune into my body and ask, "What do you need to do now?"

My body felt tired. My neck and shoulders were stiff from driving to and from Montreal for work. In fact, I'd driven around so much, I dreamed about driving.

I needed silence.

I had intended to go into town, take in my car in, stop by a museum, and so forth.

Instead, I ended up chucking my plans.

No one except me cared which day I ran all the errands.

So I didn't do it!

I rested!

Revolutionary.

But my writing seemed leaden. After I'd attended a master class with my writing mentors, Kris and Dean, in 2003, I'd committed to writing first 1000 and then 2000 words a day, every day. Even when I was on call for ICU every other night, I'd stock up words in advance so that I was always meeting my target. Through thick or thin, whether I was rotating through trauma or anaesthesia, I was writing with grim determination, like a soldier.

I only stopped when I went to the hospital for Isadora. I didn't bring my computer. I never picked up a pen. I said to myself, *You are going to live this instead of writing about it.*

But once I got home, I opened my laptop again. Two thousand words a day. Nearly all of them about Isadora.

It took me months before I tried my hand at fiction again. I wrote a short story, trying to convey my loss and longing, but I sensed that it didn't come close.

Would I ever manage to write fiction again?

I decided to e-mail Kris and ask her what she thought.

She was amazed I was writing anything at all. She said it was normal for me to dislike my fiction because real life was more crucial for me right now. I should feel free to write about Isadora, but I shouldn't force myself to write because then I'd end up hating it.

She suggested I read grief books and join a grief group. Even though I would have predicted these things intellectually, part of my brain exploded when I read that e-mail. She was saying I should nurture myself! She was saying it was okay *not* to write!

Again, it was an alien concept. Take care of myself? Tend to myself? But what about my daughter?

For the first time, though, I wrote, "Most of me believes Isadora is safe. If she is still 'here' in a way beyond my comprehension, then she is well. No one sane would punish a perfectly innocent, wondrous baby. If there is no afterlife, then she is resting. She does not know pain or sadness or irony or ugliness. She is safe.

"Which means I have to take care of me. But I'm so used to skipping over that part, paying only cursory attention to my needs. Me? Nah. I have to conceive another baby, work, lose weight, start writing, and figure out how to take care of my baby even though she's in another realm. I'm also supposed to grieve, whatever that means."

So it was okay to stop writing?

But if I stopped, what would start me back up again?

I wrote, "I'm afraid to let go of the net. It may be a trap, but it's also a secure scaffold."

Kris said all writers she knew had stopped writing while mourning, but all the committed ones started back up again.

Later, I realized that writing was a double-edged sword for me. It helped save my sanity and gave me a concrete structure to hold onto throughout what I called the "slippery, dreamy, horrid, vivid, evanescent" moods of grief. But after a while, writing became a burden, something I would force myself to do even when I was exhausted and bleary-eyed, almost a way of punishing myself.

I hung on to writing.

I hung on to my daughter.

I was very good at hanging on, at grasping and clinging. Which was exactly what Buddhism said caused suffering.

I wrote, *I cling to thee, Isadora. I cling to less appropriate things, like decade-old clothes (wait a minute! I got my Esprit T-shirt before we moved back to Canada. Next year, it will be a twenty-year-old shirt!!!!! And I still have that underwear from when I was 13!).*

The upside is, I don't give up.

The downside is, I don't give myself a break.

Could I give myself a break?

I went rollerblading. I unpinned the laundry from the line outside. I set out the garbage and recycling.

Then I picked up a non-sappy anthology about angels and read Charles de Lint's story "The Big Sky." I had read this tale before and found it good, perhaps a little predictable. But this time, I started to cry when the protagonist found a tiny baby girl in a dumpster who was afraid to move on to the afterlife. A spirit guide said, yes, it's often harder with babies, because you can't explain the afterlife to them, and they're scared.

This story captured exactly what I was afraid of. Isadora was too young, too small, too undeveloped to understand what happened. But maybe she was old enough to feel angry and bereft.

Now that I had a little girl I wanted and needed to go on to "the big sky," I read on and cried until the last page. Strange how the story had not changed, but I had changed. As the philosopher Heraclitus had observed, you can never step in the same river twice. Everything always changes.

I lay in bed, feeling tired and guilty I hadn't written yet. Tears slipped out of my eyes. Sometimes I was astonished all over again how much I still hurt and at how much I needed

Kris's—or someone's—permission that it was okay to keep on grieving.

I also needed permission that it was okay to move on.

I needed to do both, sometimes within hours or minutes of the other.

The day before, I'd been sniffing tomatoes in the grocery store to make sure they were fresh. I'd been delighted by the hibiscus flowers unfurling on the potted tree in my back yard. I wrote, "Life goes on, and I love being alive, even though my baby died. How can that be right?"

So I did what I did when the questions seemed unanswerable. I walked down to Isadora's cairn, carrying a new rock for her site. Her big vase had fallen over, so I righted it. I prayed for her.

Pema Chödrön said that she did a lot of teaching on *maitri*, or unconditional friendliness toward oneself. She said that sometimes, she thought it was the only thing she taught.

The minister, Eleanor, had asked me if I was being gentle with myself. I was still learning how to do that without abandoning my daughter.

Karma & Reincarnation

If karma ever crossed my mind before, it was just in terms of "bad karma" and "call karma."

The latter is a medical slang. One medical student could be on call for a general surgery and never get paged after midnight. Sleep for six hours. No appendectomies, no calls for Tylenol. Just sleep. Phenomenal.

Another student could be on call for gen surg for the very next 24 hours and be up all night shoving tubes down people's throats and into chests while simultaneously trying to cut out bowel cancer with his pinky finger.

We all had quiet nights and busy nights, but for whatever reason, each person tended to have an overall call karma ranging from calm or crazy. Neither extreme was ideal. You needed sleep, but you also needed enough experience so as not to kill anyone when you got out. I figured I had medium call karma.

Anyhoo, when I thought about karma before Isadora or medical school, it was mostly about bad juju and destiny. I knew that in other cultures it played a much bigger role. For example, I'd heard that in India, other people treated the "Untouchable" caste poorly and figured that they deserved it, because low caste was proof that you'd done something wrong in a previous life.

As part of my anxiety about Isadora, I worried that she'd suffered bad karma here and would now be reincarnated as an ant.

So first I polled my friends about reincarnation.

I asked one friend if she believed Isadora had been reincarnated.

"I think she's her own little soul."

The sweetness and clarity of her voice and phrasing made it sound so right to me.

I liked the idea of Isadora's unquenchable uniqueness, her soul, living forever. But I also wanted Isadora to come back again, in a different form, so she could to try out life anew.

My friend Cara seemed to believe in heaven, "but if not that, then reincarnation."

"But doesn't that mean Isadora would come back as a bug or something?"

She laughed. "I'm not sure what reincarnation means, but you might get a few attempts. If you really mess up, you come back as a lower form. But if you don't quite get it, you get to try again." Cara said it took the pressure off of her. If she didn't do right, she'd get another go round.

Leslie wrote to me about her beliefs. The soul crosses the Sea of Tears and reaches the Isle of Apples. Here, the soul rests until it becomes young again. The duration of the rest period is not related to chronological age. Then the soul can choose to return to another human body, or watch over its loved ones, or move on to other work.

I liked this concept. Isadora would be able to relax (hard work, being a baby in my tummy!) and rejuvenate herself. Then she would have options. What did she want to do? If she wanted to come back to us, we'd be eternally grateful. If she'd rather observe and protect us from another plane, I would be honoured. If she chose other parents, or flitted off somewhere, or needed more time to hang out on another plane and drink apricot nectar and watch the bees make honey, that was fine. She wouldn't be locked in to anything.

She wouldn't be trapped. She wouldn't be in pain. She would be free.

That was what I wanted for her.

Did I believe in the Isle of Apples? Not really, but I liked it enough to Google up its alternative name, Avalon. The Welsh name meant isle of apples, but I thought Avalon sounded more mysterious and lovely.

When our friend Balaji came to visit, I specifically asked him, since he'd been raised Hindu. He said he believed in reincarnation. This meant either Isadora would come back for another life, or she might never come back because she had achieved the ultimate goal, nirvana.

I said, "I like the possibility of reincarnation because I want to see her again."

"Uh huh!" He nodded vigorously, his bangs falling forward into his eyes.

"But my problem with traditional reincarnation is, I don't want her to come back as an ant."

He stared at me. "But how could she? She didn't build up any karma. She couldn't go back."

"So for sure she would be human, then, if she were coming back?"

"I'm no expert. Just remember, her concept of time may not be the same as ours."

"Why?"

"I don't know. It's just a feeling I have."

I thought about Einstein's theory of relativity. Did it apply to reincarnation?

"And anyway, what's so bad about coming back as a bug? Maybe bugs have better lives than we do."

I frowned at him. "I thought the whole idea of reincarnation is built on a hierarchy."

"It is, but I don't know if it's right. Maybe bugs are happier than we are."

I waved my hand. "I take your point, but I don't care. I don't want my daughter to be demoted in anyone's mind. So I don't want her to come back as a bug." I didn't want anyone to squish her. Heck, it could be me, squishing her!

Still, talking to my *sangha* comforted me.

For sure, Isadora didn't create any karma in my tummy. So she should come back as another human being. I knew some bereaved parents hypothesized that their "angels" would return as their next child. It was a comforting thought, but I was too much of a doubter to count on it. I'd be content as long as she was happy somewhere, someday.

I learned more about karma on about.com, through Barbara O'Brien's excellent articles.

She described karma as a dynamic process. The word means "intentional action." It's ongoing. It's always changing. Across the universe, you could think of a very complicated checks and balances sheet based on all your words and deeds.

She emphasized that your karma affected not only yourself, but everyone else, and vice versa. If all karma forms a vast sea, your karma creates ripples across the ocean that affect the other ripples.

She also said hey, the results of good karma might feel nice, but remember, your ultimate goal is to think and act while free of passion, anger, or delusion. If you hit that goal, you're not creating any karma at all, and you free yourself from this cycle of death and rebirth. That's when you end up in nirvana and get to rest.

Hindus believe in reincarnation of the soul (*atman*), but Buddha described no soul and no self (*anatman*), so different religions interpret reincarnation differently.

Barbara O'Brien suggested we think about rebirth like waves on the ocean. Any life is a wave that comes up for a bit, then turns back into the ocean.

Charlotte Joko Beck said the same thing, that our lives are like whirlpools on a river. So when we mourn someone's life passing, it makes as little sense as obsessing over a temporary swirl of water. "Wait! I really liked that whirlpool! Why's it gone now? I wasn't ready for it to go!"

Joko was obviously more detached than me. When I met my friend Leslie in person, I asked her, "Why do you think some lives are so short? Is that all there is for them? Is it so hard to bring a life into this world?"

She looked at me across the table and said, with great compassion, "I think it's both. It's very hard to cross over to this world. And then for some souls, their work is done in a very short period of time."

Attachment

I know a lot of people say, "Aw, I could never be a Buddhist. I'm too attached to stuff."

I wasn't worried about stuff, but I was still extremely attached to Isadora.

It was good that I loved Isadora so much, right? Because of all the openness, tenderness, and *bodhichitta* it engendered? But when did attachment start turning pathological?

Buddha had left his wife and newborn son in order to seek enlightenment.

One of my mom friends thought my kind of all-encompassing mother love was normal. She said she had stopped believing in God until she had kids. "Then I started thinking there had to be something, so I'd get to see them again. I'm not so worried about my husband. He's an adult. He can take care of himself. But I have to see my kids. They need me." She paused. "I was telling another friend this—I would never say it to my husband. But before, I would have said it was me and my husband plus our children. Now I'd say it was me and my children plus my husband." She laughed. "I don't know what that says about our marriage."

"No. I understand. I wouldn't have understood before Isadora, but now I do." I wiped my eyes. "There's a kind of selflessness to this love."

"It's instinctive."

The writer/artist Sark quoted one of her best friends who said, after giving birth: "This is big love."

Until now, I'd thought romance was the greatest love one could aspire to. Finding and keeping a soul mate in our great, wild world was one of the most arduous tasks one could accomplish. But I was coming to realize the love for a child was consuming and unending.

I couldn't say I loved my baby more than my husband. I couldn't compare. It just felt different. I was certain of Matt and my love. It had built up steadily over thirteen years. But the sudden grace of a child felt entirely different. A baby needed protection.

The Buddha had named his son "Rahula," which meant hindrance. He had immediately recognized that this kind of love—this kind of attachment, craving, clinging, whatever you wanted to call it—was the thing that most strongly tethered all of us to this world instead of moving on to nirvana.

I wasn't letting go of Isadora. But maybe I could figure out a way to hold on to her without losing myself.

Maybe there was a way to feel connected and opened instead of chained.

I caught a glimpse of this in an article called "Mothering as Meditation Practice," which I found at the end of the book *Buddhism for Mothers*. When writer Anne Cushman struggled with the idea of Buddha abandoning his family, she asked her teacher how Buddha could do this when he was supposed to be enlightened.

Her teacher Fu Schroeder observed, "When he left them, he wasn't the Buddha yet. He was just a confused young prince."

In my head, I imagined Anne Cushman saying, "So you think that if he'd been truly awake and enlightened then, he wouldn't have left his family?"

The teacher smiled. "Where else would you go?"

Enlightenment

"One of my students found enlightenment," said a friend at our book club meeting.

No one else responded, but I was a real "show me the money" kind of person. I said, "What exactly does that mean?"

"It means that she was meditating and she realized the oneness of everything. She saw how beautiful everything was, including a can of cola."

My book club members nodded.

I was not impressed. "Is that it?"

"No, there's more. When I see her, she says, 'How are you?' And if I'm just faking it, and I say fine, she says, 'Bull. How are you, really?'"

My book club nodded.

"That's enlightenment?" I said. I didn't think her story was as annoying as reading books about people who literally ended up seeing God, but I wasn't impressed.

I heard about one monk who meditated and saw such rapturous visions that he was convinced he was the number one rock star guru. He hiked six months through snowy mountains to tell his teacher about his wondrous achievement.

"Oh, that. That's nothing. Keep on meditating," said the teacher.

Charlotte Joko Beck said that enlightenment was just seeing life as it really was.

I returned to the ox-herding pictures for guidance. I would have assumed awakening looked a lot like panel number eight, which was a blank sheet, showing no ox and no self.

But number nine showed a scene with a tree without any human figure or an ox. It meant that life carried on and came full circle after awakening. One book said that enlightenment was part of the process. You went up the mountain and you come down the mountain. That was all.

In the book *Zen Guitar*, Philip Toshio Sudo compared the beginner's mind to a white belt in martial arts, but said that through practice, the white belt would become soiled and turn into a black belt on its own. Then, if you kept practicing, the black belt would fray until it turned into a white belt once more.

In the tenth panel, the figure dedicated herself to helping others in selfless service, while feeling complete and satisfied on her own. She could see the oneness of all things, like that a dead tree was also a sapling in bloom.

Well, I didn't expect to make it to panel number eight, ever. I still didn't get the no-self thing. But I figured my modest expectations were a good thing. I was attached to a lot of stuff, but I didn't crave enlightenment. Just a little peace and forgiveness.

Accepting What Is

(Or, My *Mono* Mother)

The Japanese have two words for "thing," *mono* and *koto*. *Mono* means an object, something you can see and touch, like a cat or a cabbage.

Koto is something you can't hold in your hand, but it makes sense in your head, like an idea, an activity, or a wish.

Martha Beck explained this concept brilliantly in her memoir, *Expecting Adam*, where she said that her in-laws were *mono* people who like to talk about airplane food, while she likes to jabber about *koto* things like primate grooming behaviours. When I read that, something clicked in my mind, but I hesitated to label my family.

"You know what we are," said my cousin Karen, right after I called her and explained the concept.

"I'm not sure."

"Come on, Mel, you know."

"Uhh ... *mono*?"

"Yes, of course we are!"

Once I had finally named it and claimed it, I felt relieved.

I had a foot in both camps. I could relate to the *mono* part. Medicine is all about *mono* and things that can be measured, like vital signs and statistical ANOVA tables.

But my soul was *koto* all the way. I loved fairy tales and preposterous ideas as much (or more than) data analysis.

Sometimes, this led to a kind of schism for me. For example, one Christian med school classmate told me about the experiment that he believed had proved the soul weighed 21 grams. He was excited that it was something you could measure.

I was like, "How does that prove anything?" I figured, either you believed or you didn't, but weighing a body before and after death probably wasn't going to sway either camp.

However, I knew one thing. My *mono* mother was never going to understand me. She was not the repository of words of wisdom or philosophical debate that would ease my heartache.

Realizing this, I was able to let it go. I would just have to go to my mother for food and my friends for conversation. There was no point in trying to force my mother to read or do yoga with me.

When another friend told me how much she hated visiting her in-laws, who spent a lot of time discussing where you could buy the cheapest tangerines, I said, "They're *mono* people." Of course, she was in the *koto* camp, someone who wanted to dedicate herself to charity and the meaning of life.

I figured either way was all right. We need both *mono* and *koto* people the make the world go 'round. We can't demand that one change into the other.

On Mother's Day, my mom surprised me with a giant wreath festooned with fake flowers and a stuffed bunny rabbit.

For me, someone who likes real flowers instead of fake and who tries not to accumulate junk, this was just about the last thing I would have picked out for myself.

Except I knew that this was her *mono* way of saying "I love you" and "You are a mother."

I said, "Thank you," and hugged her.

Oriental Medicine

I went to see a doctor of Oriental medicine after a guy at our yoga studio encouraged me to make an appointment with Dr. W. He said, "She looked at my tongue and took notes!"

I examine patients' tongues myself, mostly to assess if they're dehydrated, so that party trick didn't blow me away. "How much was it?"

"Fifty dollars."

Eventually, I decided to go for it. I didn't know much about my Chinese roots and even less about Oriental medicine, but acupuncture was an ancient and venerated tradition that couldn't hurt and might help. On the phone, I grilled her ("Do you sterilize your needles?" Answer: she used only disposable needles).

I made an appointment for a consultation. Her approach was very different from Western medicine. What impressed me was her confidence.

Instead of weighing the evidence and hoo-ing and ha-ing and consulting experts and analyzing articles, she just called 'em as she saw 'em.

When I told her I worried about my baby, she said, "Why? She is here with you."

I decided not to debate the point.

At another appointment, I said, "So many bad things are happening," and explained all the life rolls I'd been slogging through, like the dice had suddenly been loaded against me. She looked at me and said, "You are a young soul who is trying very hard to learn quickly. You have accepted this, but it means that you must suffer a lot."

In her world view, I was not doomed. I was not untouchable. I was just working through my karma.

And she was absolutely certain about her point of view.

Now, you may ask why I found this appealing when others' description of angels and heaven didn't work for me. They'd say, "Well, Isadora's an angel now," and I'd say, "What, exactly, does that mean?" I also made them explain how they envisioned heaven or what a soul was, but never left satisfied. One relative e-mailed me to say, "Everything happens for a reason." I wrote back, "Really? What is that reason?" I honestly wanted to know, but she didn't reply.

I guess, ultimately, what I liked about Dr. W's unshakable point of view was that she had a nicer story about what was happening to me.

Which made me question my own barren, self-hating version.

Was there another way to look at Isadora's short life? One that would satisfy my intellectual, rational, mono brain yet soothe my *koto* heart?

Creativity

After my mentor, Kris, had given me permission to stop writing, I still wrote about Isadora, but I approached it differently. I didn't "have" to write 2000 words. I didn't "have" to write every day. I could just see what happened.

I started reading *Walking in the World*, by Julia Cameron. I'd flipped through it before, but the references to a Great Creator did not appeal at the time. (God? Who's that?)

However, now that I was drawing comfort from the idea of Isadora's spiritual survival and transformation, I picked it up.

She suggested writing three pages longhand in the morning and three in the evening. In the morning, you could just spout off whatever you wanted, kind of like letting your thoughts roam while meditating, but writing it down instead of allowing your thoughts to fly away.

In the evening, I found it helpful to write down all the things I'd accomplished. It was just a list, but it meant that instead of going to bed mentally beating myself up for all the things I hadn't crossed off my task list, I'd think, *Hey. I managed to write 1500 words, plus I made spinach-onion casserole. Not bad.* It helped me sleep a little better.

Julia Cameron also said, at one point, "You do enough, you have enough, you are enough."

Not exactly *Om shanti* (whatever that means), but when I'd lie in bed with my heart racing, I'd think, "You do enough, you have enough, you are enough." I'd say it to myself over and over again, until my heart slowed down, and maybe I could drift off.

I was slowly discovering that, if my own thoughts depressed me, I should replace them with something else. The other thing I'd recite to myself was a line from a fortune cookie that Matt and I once broke open. That cookie contained about seven copies of the same fortune: "Happy marriage, big big house, many many children." It calmed me down.

Reading Julia Cameron and having received permission from Kris to stop forcing myself to write, I made a few small but radical changes.

Since I didn't have to count my words obsessively, I started writing in my diary again. I loved that connection between the pen and paper. I finally used a sparkly teal gel pen that I'd bought a few months ago.

I started writing for fun.

I also picked up an envelope that a friend had sent me from Singapore and began copying the elaborate design. I wasn't an artist and didn't play one on TV, but I broke out my markers and crayons and tried to imitate the tiger. It turned out better than I'd expected.

Then my "tiramisu" friend invited us to dinner the next day. First she asked me to bring fruit or drinks, but then she changed her mind and said, "Could you whip up a dessert? Yours are always so good." She ended up requesting zucchini muffins because she and her boyfriend loved zucchini. ("Strange people," said Matt.)

I grated up the zucchini for a chocolate zucchini cake. I wrote, "It's the most creative cake I've ever made. We had no eggs, so I substituted banana. We had no buttermilk, so I soured milk with vinegar. Then I decided to make it into a treasure cake to celebrate her boyfriend's birthday. My favourite birthday party cake of all time was one where a mom baked trinkets inside. A coin for wealth, a ring for marriage." Since Chipotle was a chef, my trinkets were still a ring for marriage and some coins for wealth, but I added spices wrapped in wax paper as the other treats: black peppercorn, a star anise, a small piece of cinnamon, the tip of a dried red pepper, and a green cardamom pod.

I knew that the other dinner guests might be horrified by this bizarre cake. I'd never met them before.

I wrote, *You know what? I don't give a darn. If they're such sticks-in-the-mud, let them be. They don't deserve a second chance at my magical, fortune-telling chocolate zucchini cake! It's quite a flavour explosion anyway, what with the chocolate, cinnamon, and cloves in the recipe, plus the banana. And there are treats inside. How could you resist!*

I am proud of my creativity. I may not have written a new novel since Isadora died, but gosh darn it, I'm having fun. Creative baking, drawing with crayons and markers. What next?

I came across a quote by Marianne Williamson: "Our deepest fear is not that we are inadequate. Our deepest fear is that we are powerful beyond measure. It is our light, not our darkness that most frightens us. We ask ourselves, 'Who am I to be brilliant, gorgeous, talented, fabulous?' Actually, who are you not to be?"

Slowly, slowly, I was reclaiming my creativity and my sense of humour.

Slowly, slowly, I thought it might be okay to like myself again.

Logic vs. Metaphors

My friend Leah was an atheist and a palliative care doctor, which was an unusual combination. I wondered how she consoled her patients.

She said she didn't believe in life after death except in two ways. The first was "collective memory." That didn't particularly help me, as nobody really "knew" Isadora, and my bleating "Don't forget her!" didn't trigger any more memories.

The other life after death, in Leah's mind, was biological. Even if Isadora was gone, her atoms were still around and would be made into something else. "You may encounter one of her molecules!"

I found this bizarre. "Um, I suppose that's an interesting idea, but it's zero comfort to me."

"Maybe, but isn't it more comforting than what you've been saying, that you've lost her and you'll never hold her again?"

I shook my head. Nihilism was no a cuddly bed companion, but at least it was true. "If all I wanted was her molecules, I could just cuddle up to her ashes, but I don't."

Like Leah, I had been schooled in evidence-based medicine. You practically needed a series of double-blinded, randomized control trials, based at multiple universities, free from drug company funding, before you'd dare prescribe some lip balm.

But in order for me to make some peace with Isadora's fate, I'd have to push logic aside to make room for ... not faith, not heaven, exactly, but at least the possibility that what we saw was not all that we got.

Gail Vibe wrote in her book *Sex, Soul & Synchronicity* that the male paradigm of aggression, dominance, money, and bean-counting had oppressed the female paradigm of nurturing, spirituality, intuition, and community.

Certainly I had suppressed my nurturing and ignored spirituality up until this point.

Buddhism was a non-theistic religion/philosophy, so a full-court Buddhist would side with Leah. When we died, we died. Game over.

But I had heard the Dalai Lama urge Westerners not to give up their own religious heritage to convert to Buddhism precisely because when a loved one died, or they faced their own mortality, it was too hard not to believe in the afterlife. They regretted their conversion after the fact. As the saying went, there were no atheists in foxholes and, apparently, few Buddhists on the deathbed.

I remembered one night on ICU call when I got a page from a nurse. "Bed seven has low blood pressure."

"How low?"

"You'd better come."

By the time I raced to the other side of the unit, I saw zero blood pressure on the monitor and, more to the point, her heart was in ventricular fibrillation. We could save her life, but only if we acted immediately. "It's V Fib. Shock her now!" I yelled.

They did. The patient had just had open-heart surgery. White-hot electricity arced across the staples in her chest.

Once.

Twice.

Her heart restarted. Her blood pressure returned. Her eyes flew open.

"Madame! Madame!" the male nurse cried directly into her face. *"Did you see a white light?"*

The patient nodded. She couldn't speak because of the tube in her throat.

I had to laugh. It wouldn't have been my first question.

I finished my ICU rotation a few days later, when the patient was still intubated, so I never got to ask her myself. "But she still says she saw a white light!" the same nurse reported with satisfaction.

She did see a white light, I thought. *So did I. A hundred and fifty Joules of biphasic energy arcing across her chest.*

Of course, both things were possible. She could have regained consciousness and seen the defibrillator go off a second time—and she could have had the classic near-death experience and "gone toward the light" before settling back down into her body.

One cloudy day, I prayed by Isadora's cairn and wept a little. When I returned to the house, I still felt glum. Not sobbing, just quiet and reflective and downcast, kind of like the weather.

I happened to glance out the large window panes of our back room. Suddenly, sunshine burst through the clouds and flooded our dining room table.

The scientific explanation was that the wind parted the clouds and the sun's rays reached my room.

My heart's explanation was that Isadora was saying, *Mommy, it's okay. I'm here.*

Maybe both things could be true for me, too.

The Baby Who Saved His Mother's Life

In May, the Ottawa Hospital had held a ceremony for all the babies who had died in the previous year. I invited my parents to attend. "No, thanks! We'd rather garden!" said my mother, who was already digging her shovel into the dirt.

Sigh. Breathe. Let it go.

Matt and I drove to the ceremony bearing tulips cut from our garden. We listened to songs and readings. We lit a candle for Isadora and set it among the forest of candles.

I cried so hard that salt trails dried on my face.

Afterward, I hugged our social worker. She told me to go eat something sweet. At the dessert table, a grandmotherly woman told me her daughter and son-in-law's story. I cried some more. She hugged me and said, "It's so recent for you. You should talk to my Rachel and her husband, Russ."

I felt shy. They were surrounded by friends and family already, and we were alone. But eventually, I made my way over to the couple.

I smiled at both of them. The man nodded at me and smiled from behind his thick black beard. I turned to Rachel. She had friendly brown eyes set in a heart-shaped face. "Hi. Your, ah, mother introduced herself to us."

Rachel asked, "What was your daughter's name?"

It instantly endeared her to me. Only someone else who'd gone through this knew how crucial it was to name and acknowledge your baby.

My eyes filled with tears. "Isadora. And your son?"

"Graham."

Her mother had already told me. It didn't matter. We had to exchange the names of our beloveds.

Rachel said, "It was so recent for you. How are you doing? It doesn't get better. Not really. It gets"—she held up her thumb and forefinger an inch apart—"this much easier."

I nodded. Her mother had said it had been nearly a year since Graham passed away at 39 weeks, a week before on his due date. They had never found a reason why.

"This is the worst time," Rachel said, with feeling. "I think back to how awful the first few months were, and I feel bad for you. I wish I could take it all away."

How astonishing. Her mom had told us all the layers of hell that they'd gone through, but Rachel was worried about *us*. She wanted to take *our* pain away.

She told me, "Make her box. Put a nice inscription on it."

"Did you?"

She nodded. "I'm an actor, so I chose Hamlet. 'Good night, sweet prince, / And may angels sing thee sweetly to thy rest.'"

My eyes welled up again. It was beautiful. It was heartbreaking. It was right. Unfortunately, it was an inscription best suited to a boy. I could change the word prince to princess, but it wouldn't work as well.

"There are lots of poems you can choose. It will get better. I promise. Not a lot, but a little."

When we talked on the phone later, Rachel and I compared notes.

She had been surrounded by love. People she didn't even know came to Graham's funeral. Their friends and family raised money for Russ and Rachel to go on vacation. They said, "We can't bring Graham back, but we can give you this."

Rachel did remember one woman who said, "You're lucky Graham died before he was born. It would have been much worse if he'd lived a few months."

I said, "You see the whole spectrum of human nature at a time like this, from unexpected goodness to extremely bad manners."

We agreed that we preferred to remember the good things.

Both of us had become more compassionate and less afraid of the terrible things in life. For example, her neighbour had been paralyzed in a car accident two years prior. She hadn't known what to say to her, and had found it awkward to make conversation. But now Rachel wasn't afraid to ask, "How are you doing?" or talk about her deficits.

But the thing that struck me most about Rachel's story was this:

She had worked very hard to get back in shape after delivering Graham. She'd always played soccer, but when she raced down the field and kicked the ball, she started coughing. She'd assumed it was her old asthma flaring up, but then she started coughing up more and more blood. She went to see her family doctor, who referred her to a respirologist. When they scoped her, they found that she had an unusual arteriovenous malformation (AVM, a connection between an artery and a vein) in her lung. In her case, a major artery, the internal mammary artery, was actively pumping blood into the AVM.

She could easily have bled to death.

They didn't dare try to block off the AVM the way they normally would. It was too dangerous. Nor could they excise the AVM by itself. She ended up having the middle lobe of her lung removed completely.

She said, "If Graham had lived, I would not have been playing soccer so hard. I would have been nursing him. I don't know when I would have gotten back to exercising, let alone exercising hard. The surgeon said the AVM could have ruptured any time. So I could have had a year or two with him, and then—"

She choked up.

My voice cracked. "So ... your baby saved your life?"

"*I* think so."

"That's so beautiful, I mean, sad, but beautiful." I pressed a tissue in my face. When Rachel's mother had given me the synopsis of the past year, it had been daunting. Graham had been stillborn, then Rachel had to have major, life-saving surgery. They conceived a few weeks after her surgery, but miscarried shortly afterward.

She had suffered so much, but instead of feeling sorry for herself or beating herself up for any microscopic wrongdoing, she had found something beautiful in her son's death. He didn't die for no reason. He died to save his mother's life.

It made me think of Viktor Frankl's *Man's Search for Meaning*. One day, when I felt more optimistic, I planned to read this book where he described the horror of the concentration camps. His wife, his parents, and his brother all died there. Only three percent of all the people interned survived. Frankl found that the ones who had a reason to live were more likely to make it through. To quote Nietzsche, "He who has a *why* to live can bear with almost any *how*."

Frankl himself observed, "There are two ways to go to the gas chamber: free or not free."

Rachel had faced her own set of horrors, but she had discovered meaning, love, and a reason to live.

She inspired me to head for freedom too.

Wrestling With the Angel

A few times, I'd heard the Biblical story of Jacob wrestling with an angel. They wrestled until the day broke. They wrestled until the angel touched Jacob's hip and threw it out of joint. But still, Jacob said, "I will not you go until you bless me."

The angel blessed him, but would not reveal his own name. Jacob announced afterward, "I have seen God face to face, and still I live."

This story did not resonate me at all until I heard the United Kingdom's Chief Rabbi Lord Jonathan Sacks talk about how after his father's death, he wrestled with his grief. Whenever something bad happened, he struggled and fought with his tragedy until he discovered the blessing within it.

Ah. I stood up straighter. That, I could understand.

Not "everything happens for a reason."

To the contrary, I thought a lot of things happened for no reason. As Charlotte Joko Beck put it, the rowboat was empty. The minivan hit the BMW because its brakes failed at a bad time. That was all.

Geri Larkin wrote in *The Chocolate Cake Sutra*, in every life, you get ten thousand joys and ten thousand sorrows.

So this was my sorrow. This was my most deep and devastating sorrow to date.

And, like Lord Sacks, I would battle and struggle until I extracted some sort of blessing from her death.

Samsara. Nirvana.

In *Seeds From a Birch Tree,* author Clark Strand said that a Japanese Zen master had trouble pronouncing the name Clark, so he called him "Kuraku." When it came time to give Clark a Buddhist name, he said that name was already perfect for him, because *Kuraku* means "suffering and joy" in Japanese. *Ku* and *Raku.*

Later, the master said it meant *"samsara and nirvana."*

I had heard of *samsara* before. It seemed to refer to this earthly world we lived in, full of temptation and pain.

Nirvana was a state free from suffering. It could be literally translated as "blowing out," because it meant extinguishing the triple fires of hatred, greed, and ignorance. I liked that it wasn't heaven like the traditional "you're dead, get thee to the singing angels with harps" heaven everyone else seemed okay with. This basic peace was something I could achieve here and now. Maybe.

I thought of Yvan, the professional violinist I knew who'd gone skiing and broken his arm in four places, nearly ending his career.

Yvan invited me over for lemonade. We sat on his patio, next to a young weeping willow. He told me that as far as he is concerned, on a cosmic level, human lives last such a short time, he doesn't care if a life lasts twenty weeks or a hundred years. A life is a life.

"What I want to know," he said, pouring me a glass of lemonade, "is how this has affected your medicine. How do you think you're different, as a doctor?"

I stumbled over my words. I knew I didn't like seeing pregnant women, but I also knew he wanted me to say something profound, or at least something Reader's Digest-y, about how I had finally understood the connection between Them and Me, and I looooved looking after patients now. But the truth was, I was still just doing my job, seeing patients and treating them as best I could, as fast as I could, before moving on to the next case.

I could feel his disappointment, even though Yvan politely handed me a paper towel to use as a placemat, using his good arm.

Now, years down the road, I was rereading *Seeds From a Birch Tree*. Clark Strand said that the Zen master later retranslated Kuraku to mean "sometimes *samsara*, sometimes *nirvana*." Years after that, master said, "By now, you know that your name really means *samsara* IS *nirvana*."

The first time I read this book, I was in my final year of medical school, and I probably just skimmed past these paragraphs. *Huh? How could suffering make you free from suffering?* It seemed like some weird stuff monks might say and no one else understood. "Smells Like Teen Spirit," by the band Nirvana, made more sense than that.

Today, thanks to Isadora, I finally understood the *samsara-nirvana* conundrum.

Just like Sylvia Boorstein's 40-year-old friend who died of cancer, my suffering really had transformed me and made me a better person and therefore a better doctor.

For example, the majority of kids I saw in the emerg at 2 a.m. because they woke up a stomach ache? I couldn't find anything wrong with 95 percent of them.

By the time I saw them, they were asleep in their footie pajamas. They let me push on their tummies and giggled because it tickled them. Their urine tests were clear. They didn't have a fever. They were willing to jump up and down for me. They don't look like they had appendicitis, but you never knew. So when the parents said, "Sorry for wasting your time," I'd parrot the learned doctors who taught me and reply, "No problem. We like to see your children, if you're worried." Medico-legally, you want patients to return in case it really turns out to be appendicitis, a twisted gut, a swallowed button battery, or whatever.

But now, I say these words and I'm not only worried that they're going to sue me if I miss something. I really mean it. I like kids. I like their princess- or car-bedecked pajamas. I like the way they sleep through half of the exam. I like their rounded bellies. I *care*.

By dying and ripping out my heart, Isadora had remade me into a sadder but also more joyful, alert, compassionate woman, friend, and doctor.

Rainbows and Marshmallows

One morning, as I tossed and turned, I thought at Isadora, *Are you there?*

I imagined her answering, *Yes. I'm sliding on rainbows.*

I was able to relax and fall asleep again, before I woke up and asked again, *Are you happy?*

Yes. Very happy. I'm sitting on a cloud and rubbing against a sunbeam.

A few minutes later, I asked, *Are you all right?*

Yes. I'm eating marshmallows.

I was conscious of my own mind churning out her answers, but it did make me feel better. When I'd spoken to the minister Eleanor, she'd asked if I talked to Isadora, and it twigged me that I might find it a relief to say something besides, "I love you, I miss you, I'm sorry!" and feeling the emptiness of the heavens and the unfeeling blue sky.

If I could hear Isadora's happy response, even if it was only in my own mind, and it helped me sleep better, well, why not?

Buddhism had helped me detach from my self-punishing thoughts. Now that I was creating more comforting thoughts, I was still aware that they were probably a product of my own mind rather than a psychic transmission from Isadora, but that was okay, too. Whatever worked.

So I talked to her and wrote down my version of a whole new world for her. Positive affirmations had mostly felt fake to me, but I enjoyed this and felt soothed by it. If our beliefs could actually create anything, as *The Secret* bestseller would have you believe, then my imaginary talks with Isadora could knit her a new world without care.

Maybe she was sucking her thumb, kicking her feet, and hanging out with God ("Why did you let this happen to me? I'd rather be with my Mom and Dad! ... Okay, that makes sense. When I see them again, I'll tell them.")

Maybe she was wearing a baseball cap backwards.

Maybe she pranced around naked, or clothed in clouds or bits of sky.

Maybe she was giving advice to other babies who joined her ("Here, hold my hand. You can cry as much as you want. You're a baby, aren't ya? I miss my parents, too. But they'll be here before you know it.")

I even had weird thoughts like, maybe when my breast milk dried up, it went to her in heaven. So she could have it.

Possibly, I didn't need to be as scared of death anymore. I wanted to live as long and as healthy a life as possible, with Matt by my side, but if that didn't work out, I had a baby who'd already made the trip and could show me the other side. ("I pulled a few strings to get you here, Mom, but it wasn't too hard. You're a good person. Dad will be here soon, too. I know he's still an atheist. This place will just blow him away.")

Another day, as I was driving, I felt neutral. I wrote, "Very strange. Suspended animation. Blowing neither hot nor cold." And then I had a brainwave.

Isadora was going to be fine, no matter what.

If she was in heaven, she was cruising.

If she had been reincarnated, she was figuring out a new life, no matter what form it was.

If there was no afterlife, she was resting.

No matter how you sliced it, no one else seemed to formulate an afterlife where babies suffered. One friend mentioned something about baby purgatory, but even in that strictest doctrine, our baby was blessed by a priest, so she should sweep past the staircase on that one. She was going to be all right.

My friend Leah called. I cut through the chat and said, "What do you think about us and Isadora and our future babies?" I needed reassurance.

She hesitated. "I know it's hard. I know you know these things already, so it makes it harder to tell you. But yes, I don't see any reason to worry about having more children. It's kind of better if you don't get all stressed out about having more children, because it doesn't help. It's probably better if you have this time when it's just you and Matt and Isadora. When you have your next pregnancy, it'll be better if it's not all about that."

It was a nicer way to think about it, me and Matt and Isadora, instead of just the two of us, barren and bereft of our baby.

Leah liked the idea of Isadora hanging out with the rainbows. She said she just doesn't know about the afterlife, and if there was any time it was useful to think of there being a hereafter, it was now.

I nodded. I felt better. I even smiled to myself a little and thought, *So another atheist begins to yield.*

She said, "Why not give yourself the benefit of the doubt? When patients are in comas, we tell their families to talk to them. Maybe they can hear. We don't know whether they can or not, but often there are so many unresolved issues, the kindest thing is to encourage the family to talk to the patient. At worst, it brings the family some sort of comfort. At best, all is heard and forgiven."

"That makes sense. Thanks."

Afterward, I wrote, "I have traveled such a long and thorny path, I deserve some solace. So Isadora, hip hop angel guide to the heavens, sounds darn good to me."

Buddhist or Just Buddhish?

Susan Piver, author of *How Not to Be Afraid of Your Own Life*, explained Buddhism very simply. Buddhists were people who could say:

> I take refuge in the Buddha (wakefulness).
> I take refuge in the *dharma* (wisdom).
> I take refuge in the *sangha* (community).

I thought about the last one first, because it was easier. I had my mustard seed *sangha*, Matt and Olo and a scattered but committed group of wise friends who supported me through the grace of the telephone and the Internet. One of them said, "I'm worried about you! You're all alone out here!" because we had recently moved to the country. But actually, I was building a *sangha* here too.

I wrote, *I feel surrounded by goodness.*

When we moved in, one neighbour greeted us with apple pie. Another led Olo home if he strayed and offered to drive me to the hospital if I needed it. Father Dan was terrific, really a gem. More neighbours invited us to our first corn roast and still others to our first Robbie Burns Day. One couple mowed our hay and fixed our car. I'm slowly getting to know all the people, and they have good, helpful hearts.

I really feel like I'm part of a community. It helps buoy me up. Julia Cameron firmly believes the universe will help you fulfill your creative endeavours. I haven't seen it bear a lot of fruit for me so far, for my writing. But in general, I feel like there is great benevolence around me.

The emergency room is not a great place to feel optimistic about human spirit. People are hurting. If they're not screaming in pain or hemorrhaging or having a heart attack in front of you, they often have to wait hours and hours and resent you for it.

But I met some good souls on the weekend, starting with an elderly man who'd been waiting since 9:30 a.m. for constipation and felt embarrassed about it, 'but I have to look after myself.' I had such an urge to hug him. Next time, I might give in to it.

Another father was genuinely grateful, even though his 16-year-old daughter with a sore ear and throat was like, 'Let's go.' Actually, I got the feeling that the father found me attractive, but anyway. The point was, he wasn't making passive-aggressive comments or demanding pointless antibiotics.

So, at home and even at work, I had the *sangha* part pretty much nailed down.

Did I take refuge in the *dharma*, the wisdom spoken and written and demonstrated around me?

I thought so. My whole life, I'd enjoyed observing and reflecting. The bumper sticker I'd pasted on the bottom of my laptop said, "Shut your mouth. Open your mind." Now that I'd lost Isadora, I was even more wide open to hearing people's experiences before making up my own mind.

Maybe I wasn't wise, but I was open to wisdom. Pema Chödrön suggested that instead of judging, we should just be curious. I'd always been curious.

What about the Buddha? Not necessarily the person, but the idea of being awake and present in every moment?

Probably not. I still didn't really meditate. Sometimes, during corpse pose in yoga, or just before falling asleep, I might think *Peace, peace* or *I am enough*.

But I was much more attuned to the present moment than I had been. I might not listen to the metal clothes hangers ring together when I grabbed my blouse for the day, but I did look up at the clouds when I stopped at a traffic light. I did pause for a second during my emergency room shift to take a sip of orange juice and feel grateful for its sweet citrus tang.

Julia Cameron maintained that writing was a legitimate form of meditation. If so, I was meditating through writing again. Sometimes I kicked it old school and let my pen rip across the page. Just like in the past, no matter if it was handwritten or on the computer, I usually achieved a sort of no-self, no-care state, banging on the keys like I was downloading thoughts from another plane. I even might try to break out a made-up story one of these days.

I wrote, *These are my meditations. These are my thoughts rippling across the page. This is my life now.*

I thought of the Eightfold Path, where Right Thinking naturally flows into Right Action and the rest of it. I wrote, *By looking after myself and my emotional and spiritual needs, I can step more firmly in the world, achieving what needs to be done.*

It is not selfish. It is an inherent part of my role. I can't just help, help, help without looking to myself. I would become empty and irritated. I have to refill the well. That means spending quiet, quality time with myself.

So, was I a Buddhist now?

Ech. My meditation was still very lame.

So. Buddhish.

I was fine with that. Buddhism and Buddhish-ism were just labels. The most important part was how I felt. I wrote, "Overall, I still feel like the world is a strong and beautiful place to live."

Cinderella

Whenever I read books about other women who'd lost babies, or met these women in real life or online, I looked for the Cinderella ending: more children. At least one more, maybe several.

Then I'd feel simultaneously hopeful ("Maybe I can have more kids too!") and annoyed ("It only took her a month before she was preggo again. I can't relate").

If someone spun a traditional story about me, I figured the Cinderella ending would be for me to find Yahweh somewhere and get pregnant again, culminating in a line like, "On [this date], Melissa and Matt welcomed a healthy baby [boy/girl/both]." So readers could close the book and sigh with relief that at least it turned out all right in the end, as it should.

As part of getting to know and accept myself, though, I realized it was okay that I still wasn't convinced if a god or gods existed. It was still okay not to believe in any one thing. It was also okay not to be totally Buddhist.

But maybe the other fairy tale ending was within my grasp. Because one day, half a year after I delivered Isadora, I wrote, "So far, it's 7:26 p.m. and still no period."

My friend Beatrice e-mailed me back. "Cautious optimism. But if not this cycle, the next one."

I felt stronger than that. I had a good feeling about it.

Of course, my old pal, restlessness, knocked on my door. Even before I took a pregnancy test, I worried if Isadora might feel displaced by a new life inside me.

My more cynical friends might say, *You'll have other children. You'll get bogged down in nap times and play groups and the best preschools and you'll forget.*

I didn't think so. Isadora was a seismic shift in my life. She claimed a portion of my heart. Leah's grandmother was 90 years old, but she still mentioned her firstborn and only son who died, even though she had four girls afterward.

It was like the line in *The Princess Bride*, when The Man in Black said something like, "I know *I* can't survive death. But true love can. It does all the time. Don't you know that?"

I went in-line skating, which made me feel groovilicious. Then I walked down to say hi to Isadora and pray for her. Her little blue spruce and one out of two cherry trees looked good.

I started to cry.

It wasn't logical. No one else thought she'd be angry at us for having another baby. I had enough room in my heart for her and ten other babies. We would have wanted more than one child anyway. But I still worried that she would resent a brother or sister, or, more importantly, us, for "moving on" and away from her.

I realized this meant that I was worried about it myself. I realized that these were just thoughts.

I placed my left hand on my tummy. In my right hand, I clutched some red roses and shook the loose petals around her cairn while I walked and prayed for her eight times, "May you be happy. May you be free from suffering."

For the next eight times, I prayed, "May we be happy. May we be free from suffering." I thought of the potential life in my belly. Even though I hadn't confirmed it yet, I figured that now or at some point in the future, I needed to work on this guilt about our (fingers crossed) many, many children.

Lastly, I prayed, "May all beings be happy. May all beings be free from suffering."

It helped.

Little Miracles

Matt and I flew to Oahu. We surfed in the wild waters of Waikiki. I dragged him to a yoga retreat on the Big Island. And, the day before my birthday, I woke up at 3 a.m., after six and a half hours of sleep. But I felt awake.

I took my temperature. 36.7 degrees Celsius.

Aww. That was a little lower than the morning before. But if I'd slept in another hour, it would probably nudge up to 36.8 and therefore be okay. If I walked around and it popped up to 37, that would seem even more like a higher temperature consistent with conception, but it would no longer be a resting temperature.

Hang on. For the first time, I had not woken up to pee in the middle of the night. I was now awake and I still did not have to go.

Oh no! Two possible signs that I might not be pregnant!

Yet as long as my period stayed away, I was most likely with child.

Or I could stop all this living and dying by my temperature and fluctuating symptoms each morning and take the darn test.

I was nearly five weeks pregnant by dates. That should be good enough for a positive pregnancy test.

I lay there, undecided. What if it was negative? Wouldn't it spoil my birthday?

But worrying at 3 a.m. was also spoiling my birthday and my vacation.

My heart knocked in my chest. I was afraid.

I sat up and pushed back our bed's mosquito netting. I slid my feet onto the floor and rummaged through my suitcase for the drugstore pregnancy test. Then I slid the pocket door of the bathroom closed and peed on the stick.

I was afraid to look. But almost right away, the first window started to blush.

My heart grew wings.

Two lines. Pregnant.

I just sat there and whispered, "Thank you, thank you, thank you, thank you, thank you" until I ran out of breath. I had tears in my eyes.

I was thanking the Great Spirit, whatever form it might take. But, even more intimately for me, I was thanking Isadora. This was the first month I'd asked for her help in getting pregnant. Before, I'd wanted to take care of her, not ask her for any boon. But this past cycle, I'd felt like it was too big a burden for me. I needed her help. I went to her cairn and asked for it, if she was willing to give it.

And she had delivered.

I thought at the new life inside me, *Hello, baby. I knew you were there, but it's nice to have something else say so, too.*

This baby was not going to replace Isadora. I searched my heart and realized that, at this juncture, I loved Isadora more than I loved the new baby. To be fair, I didn't love her yet either when she was brand new. I hadn't known she existed until I realized I was a few weeks late, and then, since we vacationing in Costa Rica, I'd waited until we'd flown back to Canada to take the test. Afterward, I was so afraid of losing her, I probably didn't really fall in love with her until I got my first ultrasound and she wiggled her arms at me.

I figured I'd love this baby sooner because Isadora had paved the way. Maybe I already loved him/her/it and was afraid to let myself go.

I crawled back in bed to tell Matt. He hugged me in his sleep.

I whispered, "It's confirmed."

Blearily, he dragged out, "What?"

"Preggie-weggie." (I'm embarrassed to admit it, but I used to baby talk to Matt sometimes.)

He patted my hip.

I said, "I love you."

"I love you."

"I love Isadora."

"What?"

"I love Isadora."

He nodded, eyes still closed. "Me too."

"I love this new baby."

He nodded and murmured something.

"Are you happy?"

"Yes." He rolled on his back.

I wanted more. "Why?"

Pause. "Why not?"

I knew he was asleep, but c'mon. "Are you happy about the new baby?"

Pause. "I'll have to finish the floor." He meant installing the hardwood floor in the nursery.

I lay down beside him and stared at the mosquito netting. I smiled. Matt was never going to send out sky rockets and balloons over my positive pregnancy test. When I told him I was pregnant with Isadora, he'd said, "Uh huh" and kept playing fetch with Olo. Later, he said he'd have to finish the hardwood floor. Just like this time.

About two months after we'd returned from our vacation in Hawaii and I was waiting for my first ultrasound, I reflected again on the saying, "Ten thousand joys, ten thousand sorrows."

A lot of the Buddhist books talked about how every single one of us wanted the joy. Happy happy, joy joy, Snoopy dance, wahoo, w00t w00t! But when the sorrow cropped up, as it inevitably did, you felt isolated. You felt ashamed of your bad luck. It didn't matter if you'd lost your job or if a family member had committed suicide. You were shut away twice, once by grief and a second time by shame.

I'd considered myself a burden. I'd avoided calling any one of my friends too often because I was afraid I'd be too much for each individual.

Luckily, doctors and nurses and hospital staff, as a tribe, understood that ten thousand sorrows happened to everyone. They didn't shy away from danger and heartache. In fact, they may rush in to help. Also, I had enough friends that I could kind of rotate through them and they would sustain me.

Tonight, instead of going to bed, I went on babyworld.com and read about British celebrities' pregnancies. I took a quiz to see who I was more like. It turned out to be someone I'd never heard of who had a quite normal pregnancy (felt "knackered," ate a lot).

It cheered me up. Other people might read about celebrities in order to drool over their material possessions, handsome co-stars on- or off-stage, or easy lifestyle ("I only worked 11 weeks last year," said Kate Winslet, "and most of the time, my daughter was with me"), but I envied their sweet little babies. It gave me hope I could live out that particular fantasy.

I decided to go and pray to Isadora in the morning.

When I woke up, I considered cutting the last, hardiest flowers and bringing them to her cairn. The first frost had hit this past week, but the temperatures still sometimes ventured above freezing during the day. Yet any flowers wouldn't survive long. Plus the last time, I had ensconced her vase in her cairn, but the rocks had dropped out, and the vase had tipped over. Matt had warned me about the water freezing and breaking the vase. Maybe it was just as well if I let the decorations go.

In a way, it simplified things. I walked down the hill without water or clippers or new flowers. Just myself, with Olo bounding ahead of me.

I circled the cairn and prayed. When I finished, I asked Isadora for help.

I felt guilty, like the time I asked her for help getting pregnant. It seemed so backwards. I was the mother. She was a baby. I should be taking care of her, not requesting favours. She would only be about four months old on earth.

But the non-logical, intuitive part of me argued, *If her spirit lives, she's more than a baby. She's more than I can ever conceive of here. She exists on another plane. She knows goodness and sweetness and sees further into the distance.*

I asked for Isadora's help to keep this baby healthy.

My rational side rolled its eyes. If Isadora had any power over healing, she should have made sure she was healthy and alive and with us now.

But she wasn't with us. And maybe it meant she got some sort of backstage pass. I needed to believe that she had access to a divinity beyond our grasp.

I told Isadora, *I still can't really imagine one God. I have even more trouble worshiping Jesus or any other prophet. But I will always believe in you.*

Christians said that God sent Jesus as an intermediary between Himself and us, so we could better grasp holiness when we saw it in human form.

I thought of Isadora as my little intermediary. My miniature spirit guide.

It was funny. When I was a kid in school, studying Indigenous beliefs, I never had any trouble with depictions of Mother Earth, Mother Creator, or Father Lightning. They made intuitive sense to me. If you linked the divine with the earth, all you had to do was look around and see goodness, nurturing, and miracles. Like on the show *Joan of Arcadia*, Joan said to God, who took relatively random human forms, "Fine. Show me a miracle." The guy pointed at a tree. She said, "That's a tree." He said, "Let's see you make one."

Trees.

Rainbows.

Wet, squelchy earth.

Weak winter sun and full-tilt summer sunshine.
Water fountains.
The curve of a mountain.
Autumn sky so blue it hurts, framing the last branch of the crab apple tree.
A Christmas cactus blooming early.
A grain of sand.
The tide.
A fish.
Balance.
Surfing.
The perfect curve of blue pottery.
A fresh muffin filled with melting chocolate chips.
Bread straight from the oven.
A tomato sandwich when you're starving.
Olo.
Marrying the love of your life.
Chocolate raspberry torte.
Starting a fire on a cold, damp day.
Sleeping in with Matt.
Walking, running, rollerblading.
Holding a pose in yoga and knowing your body, your mind, and your balance.
A good night's sleep.
This baby in my belly.
The baby who came and had been returned to the embrace of the earth.
Real, true friendship.
Dawn and sunset.
Lying still.
Reading a wonderful book.
Rereading an even more wonderful book.

These were all little, everyday miracles.

People said to count your blessings because we seemed to excel at grouching instead.

It did help me to list them. It gave me hope.

There was goodness in the world. I always knew it. I hoped there would be more good news in store for this wee, vulnerable babe.

Heal Thyself

Buddhism emphasized healing oneself in order to help save the world.

I struggled with this. Shouldn't I work on helping to save gorillas or preserve the rainforests?

Did it really matter what I did?

When I was in my 20s, I suddenly realized that most people didn't give a flying fig about me. They were so consumed by the minutia of their own lives ("I bought a car!" "Do you think I'm fat?") that they didn't give anyone else more than a second's attention.

That was liberating. It let me do what I wanted, knowing that I didn't rate too high on the general population's radar.

A few years later, I realized the opposite: I did have an impact. Patients or their families told me how grateful they were to see me, even if I hadn't done too much for them. Before, they might have asked if I had a practice outside the emergency room, and I'd think, *Oh, yes, everyone needs a family doctor.* But I came to realize that some of them really appreciated me. Not anyone who had a pulse and a stethoscope. Me.

That helped me, too, to know that I mattered.

Sharon Salzberg wrote a wonderful story about how she wanted to help Aung San Suu Kyi, the Burmese leader for democracy who was under house arrest for fifteen years. Sharon felt helpless. How could she help this brave woman when even the Nobel Peace Prize and the United Nations had failed to release her from the claws of the military dictatorship? Years later, Suu Kyi wrote to Sharon, thanking her for her book on meditation. Sharon's book had made it past the invisible prison bars. By simply doing her work, Sharon had made a difference to Suu Kyi.

Bhante Y. Wimala explained it like this:

A teacher wanted to teach his students that if you want world peace, you have to start with yourself.

His students were confused. They liked peace, sure, but weren't they just a handful of kids in a world of seven billion people? What difference did they make?

The next day, teacher brought in a puzzle with a map of the world. The students laboured over it, but it was hard to piece together each scrap of land or fragment of the ocean when everything seemed to meld together.

"Stop," said the teacher, after a few minutes. "Would you like to see an easier way to put the puzzle together?"

They turned the puzzle pieces over and saw the reverse side made a picture of a man. This was much easier. They knew how to assemble the eyes, the nose, and so on. They finished it easily.

When they turned the puzzle over, they realized that they had put together the map of the world without even realizing it.

By telling my story, I know that other people will criticize me. They will say my story doesn't matter, that Isadora was not even a real baby, and that I have no right to complain.

I will answer that she is my baby and that I love her. That she mattered to me. That I will complain if I want to, but mostly I just want to remember her and let you know that if you are hurting, too, it's all right. I wanted to tell you that if you can piece yourself together, one fragment at a time, it's not only necessary and good for you, but for the whole world.

May you be happy. May you be free from suffering.
May I be happy. May I be free from suffering.

May all beings be happy. May all beings be free from suffering.

Peace.

Epilogue (Meditation 3.0)

I did manage to keep that delicious baby. His name is Max. My husband and I had debated over the names Maxwell and Jasper, but as soon as I saw his face, I thought, *It's Max!* We flipped a coin (Matt didn't want to, but I said it was fine. I was sure that Max would win. And it did. Since then, a few friends told me they were glad, because Jasper is a dog's name).

Soon after Max was born, my dad came to visit, and he said he was having trouble with his memory.

"Do you want me to scan your head?" I said. It was a bit awkward, because now I was on maternity leave from my hospital in Quebec, but I knew I could arrange something in Ontario, if I had to.

"No. My doctor referred me to a memory clinic," he said, and I got the feeling that he wanted me to be his daughter instead of his doctor, so we cooed over Max, and I later asked my brother to keep an eye on him.

My brother called me in a panic six months later. My father had stumbled on a word while practicing for a job interview. He didn't have a seizure, but he could not say the correct word.

"We need to rule out a mass," said my neurology friend, and I arranged an urgent neurology appointment and CT scan. My brother drove Dad to Cornwall. And there we discovered a very deep brain tumor in Dad's brain, requiring an MRI that night. Neither the neurologist nor the radiologist wanted to tell my dad, so I sat him and my brother down and did it.

"I'd like to stay and see this one grow up," Dad said, waving his hand at Max, who had fallen asleep in his stroller. "But I've done what I needed to do. Take care of Mom."

Ten thousand joys, ten thousand sorrows. It seemed like as soon as I held my heart's desire, a healthy baby, life stabbed me again with my father's cancer. And my mother-in-law's premature dementia. And a miscarriage. And Olo got cancer too—

I chronicled those events in other books. In the meantime, I can tell you that we survived those years. Well, actually, my dad, my mother-in-law, and Olo did not survive, but Matt and I were eventually able to give Max a little sister.

My *mono* mother became more *koto* in that she reads more books, including fiction, which she used to scorn. (Her favourite novel of mine is *Wolf Ice*, the one teeming with sex and werewolves!)

And a few events in my life have conspired to make me meditate more.

First of all, I have dry eyes, so I have to spend about ten minutes a day covering them with a warm, wet compress to help lubricate them. It's hard to zoom around with a blindfold on. I've tried to spend the downtime doing yoga on my back, or listening to podcasts, but every so often, I end up meditating. Something about lying in enforced darkness, with a physical weight over my eyes, tells me that it's okay to lie still without accomplishing anything external.

Secondly, our family has started karate. Yes, Max turned eleven and has a huge predilection for video games. That means we all need to get more active, and since the local dojo charges the same after two family members, Matt, Max and I are learning how to grapple and kick while Max's sister watches. It is an exercise in humility most of the time. However, one un-advertised part of the practice is that we start off and end with meditation.

It's the only time I meditate with my family and with a larger group, and a stark contrast to the rest of the class: we could be beating each other up minutes before, but then we gather together on the mat and meditate. I kind of like it.

Thirdly, now there are apps. I'm a late adopter to this. I mostly use my phone at the hospital, to calculate drug dosages, so every time I touch my phone outside of work, I feel compelled to wash my hands. It's not a pocket-sized piece of fun, the way it is for everyone else. But I'm exploring meditation apps, partly because when I drive home from the ER after an evening shift, my mind is still racing: *Did I chart that? I didn't see enough patients. That guy was rude to me*...and I don't get to sleep for hours after my shift has ended. Even if it takes me 45 minutes or less to drive home, I'm still edgy, hyper, and wound up, so either I don't get to sleep, or I wake up hours early, which cuts my energy the next day.

Then a revelation struck me: maybe if I meditated on the way home, I could mentally downshift during the drive, and by the time I hit the doorstep, I wouldn't have to unwind as much. Meditation could make me more efficient.

Last night, I cued up some meditation audio for my 1.5 hour drive home, and it definitely helped. Just the background sound of water and birds twittering subconsciously made me relax. I found myself noticing that it was dark outside at 10 p.m. Not a revolutionary observation, but the blackness enveloped me. I noticed it, and thought, yes, it's time to go to bed. The world is on my side, working its magic, carrying me toward sleep. Cars whooshed by, their headlights sweeping the darkness, and I observed them calmly.

The only downside? I suddenly felt tired and wanted to go to sleep. Dangerous when you still have another hour to go. But I made it home, patted my barking dog, unpacked my supper, and dropped off for a good eight hours. And, as the Dalai Lama himself said, "Sleep is the best meditation."

Appendix: Buddhist Books I Love

It's Easier Than You Think, by Sylvia Boorstein. I find her so accessible, down-to-earth, and honest. Like a Jewish grandmother hugging you along the path to Buddhism.

Zen Shorts, by Jon Muth. The children's book I never get tired of reading to my son. Wise, funny, beautifully illustrated.

Writing Down the Bones, by Natalie Goldberg. This was my first introduction to Zen at age 18, by Dr. Sylvia Bowerbank at McMaster University. Not only did this book free me up to write, but certain Zen ideas still pop into my mind regularly. Goldberg's main teacher, Katagiri Roshi, was the one who said he didn't let loneliness toss him away. Simple but profound. Similar to what the Dalai Lama said about anger. Roshi also mentioned the idea of fighting the tofu, or battling uselessly and struggling mightily, only to achieve nothing.

The Chocolate Cake Sutra, by Geri Larkin. Once I got past the first few pages, I dove in and consumed this book and bought her entire backlist. She talked about how her Detroit abbey was plagued by rats. Everyone said to shoot them or poison them, but since that went against the principle of non-violence, they brainstormed and came up with a different solution: clean up all the garbage. Where there was no garbage, there were no rats. So they took on this laborious, slow task, and it worked. I also loved the "crazy wisdom" of one of her colleagues. Geri Larkin held a fundraiser where you could ask this woman anything, and she answered everything from "How do you manage to pray when you have four children underfoot?" and "I'm not supposed to be attached to earthly things, but my first baby is about to be born, and I already can't imagine my life without her."

Things Fall Apart, by Pema Chödrön. It made me see things in a deeper way. Nearly every mini essay made me pause to think. For example, how does maitri (loving-kindness toward the self) help the world? And, as in all books I can relate to, she doesn't pretend to be all that. When her husband told her he was leaving her, she threw a rock at him. But she emphasizes that all crises are an invitation to soften and develop insight.

Everyday Zen: Love and Work, by Charlotte Joko Beck. Blew me away. She challenged my ideas about how I approach writing and other former pleasures. By trying to compete with other people's writing success and turning it into work instead of a joy, I nearly ruined it.

Lovingkindness: The Revolutionary Art of Happiness, by Sharon Salzberg. Chock-full of goodness, but I especially remember her comparison of dropping a teaspoon of salt into a cup vs. into the ocean. Everyone's like, Noooo! Not the salt! Keep that salt away from me! But you can't alter the salt (death, illness, other crappy stuff) as easily as you can modify what it spills into (your mind). Meditation and mindfulness allow you to become more like the ocean that can better accept the salt instead of the cup of water.

Mountains Are Mountains, Rivers Are Rivers: Applying Eastern Teachings to Everyday Life, edited by Ilana Rabinowitz. If you want a one-stop book with wisdom culled from a bunch of different authors, including a few of the writers listed above, this one delivers. You know how a few pages can pack a bigger punch than an entire tome? Ilana Rabinowitz made sure to pick out the best.

How Not to Be Afraid of Your Own Life: Opening Your Heart to Confidence, Intimacy, and Joy, by Susan Piver. A book of Buddhism in the world of jeans and cell phones. If Sylvia Boorstein is your Jewish grandmother, Susan Piver is like your adorable, insecure but wise girlfriend who listens to you after you slept with your impossible ex-boyfriend—but points you in the right direction afterward.

When I was writing this book, one of my beta readers suggested that the general public might not be interested in Isadora and that I should take her out in order to increase reader appeal. But to quote Susan Piver's teacher, Sakyong Mipham Rinpoche, if you want to present a spiritual teaching, you must first "create confidence in the mind of the person studying it. The way to create confidence is to offer something real." My experience of Isadora is one of the real-est things I know. Obviously, I kept her in.

Meditation Apps

You don't need an app to meditate. You can just be still and close your eyes, or walk mindfully. But if you're constantly distracted and running around like me, you might want to try these. I'm a beginner on all of them and have not yet upgraded past any pay wall.

Headspace
Cute cartoons. A bright orange background. A narrator with a British accent. This is an app with personality. The meditations are so short, at only three minutes, that even I thought they could go a bit longer. This is a great place to start if you're more ADHD.

Simple Habit
Dark colours, soothing voice, straightforward narration. They want you to set a time to meditate every day, which is a good idea if you're not a shift worker like me. To be honest, I could probably get it to set a time where I'd meditate if I'm not working—I'm just not there yet. I don't like how it defaults to some sort of overview screen after you finish the meditation, but overall, this is an easy, classy app.

Calm
I love the background bird twittering and water rushing. I liked the free content, and the idea of picking out a theme (I always pick "sleep"). I also listened to a sleep story, because I would enjoy someone reading to me at bed time.

Non-Buddhist But Still-Useful Resources:

Dojo Wisdom for Mothers, Dojo Wisdom, and Dojo Wisdom for Writers, by Jennifer Lawler. Quick, simple, but profound pages. Jennifer Lawler had been overweight and suffering from rheumatoid arthritis before she discovered martial arts. It saved her life. And it saved her life again when her daughter was born with tubular sclerosis because Jennifer had learned mental clarity as well as physical skills. I bought the first book after I opened it and read a quote from a female Supreme Court Justice, who was asked how she balanced work and family. She replied, "I have a brain and a uterus and I use both."

The Joy Diet, Finding Your Own North Star, and Steering by Starlight, by Martha Beck. I love her wry, self-deprecating, but confident voice, and I love what she has to say. For example, she says to give yourself three treats a day. That means anything that makes you smile. Her high-powered clients say, "Well, I guess I could exercise more." Martha says, "Mmm, nope. A real treat."

Yoga Today, yogatoday.com. I've been doing yoga since before Madonna and Lulu Lemon, and this site lets me watch three different teachers teach classes on different levels. I still tend to rush through the breathing at the beginning (my bad), but I love being able to try a few class for free, at home, on my own time. I bought a subscription because I learn from them. During one class, I realized that yoga is a form of prayer and meditation for me. It's a time where I can clear the chattering of my mind and just be present and send well-wishes. During a class with the theme of ahisma (non-violence), I realized that worrying was actually a form of violence against myself. Slowly, I try to un-learn that habit.

Fightmaster Yoga, https://www.youtube.com/user/lesleyfightmaster/playlists. There are so many good, free yoga teachers on YouTube. You should find one who speaks to you. I like Lesley Fightmaster because she tries things that are different and challenging (borderline impossible) for me, yet has a sense of humor, like dressing up like a witch on Hallowe'en. I also find it soul-enriching to join a local yoga studio and meet people who care.

On Being podcasts, NPR. Krista Tippett interviews scientists, poets, spiritual leaders, parents of autistic children, all ordinary and extraordinary people, asking them how they see spirituality in their world. She talked to Waagiri Maatai, the Kenyan woman who planted 30 million (30 million!) trees with the help of rural women. Maatai was imprisoned for her efforts, but won the Nobel prize and kept on planting. I loved hearing about how indigenous Kenyan spiritual beliefs, her Catholic upbringing, and her Ph.D. in the U.S. during the turbulent 1960s all helped influence her. It reminded me of the Buddhist response to all the violence and chaos surrounding us: plant a tree. And I decided that instead of struggling to find the perfect Christmas or gifts for families who have everything, I would give them a tree. They may hate it. The tree may die. But I will give them a tree anyway.

The Essential Rumi, by Jalal al-Din Rumi and translated by Coleman Barks. Clear, musical, sometimes contradictory wisdom. You could open this book randomly and let yourself ponder whichever poem catches your eye.

Your Baby Is Safe, by Melissa Yuan-Innes and D. Antonia Truesdale. One last note about one of my own books, which is not explicitly Buddhist. I wrote almost half a million words about Isadora. In the end, I distilled them to just 400 words that I wished other people had said to me. I called the book Your Baby Is Safe. I envisioned it as a picture book for adults. I knew there was a market for this, since Rachel had sent me a book called *Mommy, Please Don't Cry*, which was written for Christian moms, but I wanted mine to appeal to parents with various belief systems.

I sent it out to numerous publishers, none of whom saw it as a profitable venture, although a few said they were sorry for my loss.

I kept sending it out. I wrote, "No one puts my baby in the corner." But I never did find a market.

Then one day, years later, twiddling around on Etsy.com, I discovered The Midnight Orange. I saw D. Antonia Truesdale's round, touching, yet sometimes dark sculptures, and I knew her art, her spirit, and her heart were exactly right for my book.

Your Baby Is Safe is now available as a paperback and an ebook.

When reviewing an advance copy, Maggie McVay Lynch, Ed.D., wrote, "The words and imagery are wonderful .... I hope it provides many people with some comfort and thought."

Thank you for reading. If you enjoyed this book, I would be most grateful if you could let a friend know and post a positive review.

Namaste.
Melissa
www.melissayuaninnes.com

www.ingramcontent.com/pod-product-compliance
Lightning Source LLC
LaVergne TN
LVHW041219080426
835508LV00011B/997